Preaching from Luke/Acts

Editors
David Fleer and Dave Bland

Preaching from Luke/Acts

A·C·U
PRESS

ACU Box 29138
Abilene, TX 79699
www.acu.edu/acupress

Cover Design and Typesetting by Sarah Bales

David Fleer and Dave Bland, editors

Printed in the United States of America

ISBN 0-89112-135-8

Library of Congress Card Number: 00-108509

1,2,3,4,5

TO DEBBIE FLEER FOR HER AFFIRMING LOVE AND

UNFAILING ENCOURAGEMENT

AND

TO NANCY BLAND FOR HER UNTIRING GIFT

OF MINISTRY

TO HER FAMILY AND OTHERS.

Acknowledgments:

Thanks to Mike Westerfield, Jennifer Hamilton, and Chris Altrock
for their close reading of the early manuscripts and
to Ken Johnson, President of Rochester College, for his
pioneering spirit in support of the Sermon Seminar
and the essays it has inspired. Thanks to our editor,
Charme Robarts for carefully working the book through
its final stages to completion.

Table of Contents

Biographical Sketches

Dave Bland served for ten years as the pulpit minister for the Eastside Church of Christ in Portland, Oregon. Currently, he is one of the pulpit preachers for the White Station Church of Christ in Memphis, Tennessee. He is Associate Professor of Preaching at Harding University Graduate School of Religion in Memphis. He completed the M.Div. from Abilene Christian University, the D. Min. from Western Seminary, and the Ph.D. from University of Washington.

David Fleer served as the pulpit minister for churches in Vealmoor, Texas and Vancouver, Washington and has worked as an interim minister for churches in Oregon and Michigan. He is currently Professor of Religion and Communication at Rochester College. He completed the M.Div. from Abilene Christian University, the D.Min. from Fuller Theological Seminary, and the Ph.D. from the University of Washington.

Timothy W. Kelley has served as a minister for the following California churches: Roseville Church of Christ, Whittier Church of Christ, Torrance Church of Christ, Morro Bay Church of Christ, and currently, Camarillo Church of Christ. He completed the Master of Arts degree in Religion at Pepperdine University.

Thomas G. Long is the Bandy Professor of Preaching at Candler School of Theology in Atlanta. He has also taught at Columbia Theological Seminary and at Princeton Theological Seminary and has served as director of Geneva Press for the Presbyterian Publishing Corporation. His books include The *Witness of Preaching, Preaching and the Literary Forms of the Bible*, and commentaries on Hebrews and Matthew.

Dean Smith is the preaching minister for the University Church of Christ in Austin, Texas and an adjunct faculty member at the Institute for Christian Studies (Austin), teaching courses in ministry and preaching. He is a graduate of Rochester College and McCormick Theological Seminary.

Greg Sterling has served for the last ten years as the Associate Professor of New Testament and Christian Origins at Notre Dame and is the Director of Graduate Studies. Sterling is the pulpit minister for the Warsaw Church of Christ and author of *Historiography and Self-Definition: Josephus, Luke-Acts and Apologetic Historiography* and, *Prayers and the Ancient World*, forthcoming.

John O. York currently serves as one of the preaching ministers of the Woodmont Hills Church of Christ in Nashville, and he is associate professor of Bible and preaching at Lipscomb University. He previously worked with congregations in Oregon, Texas, and Tennessee and served on the faculty of Columbia Christian College. He holds a Ph.D. in New Testament from Emory University.

Foreword

It is difficult to preach upon biblical texts in an incisive, engaged and passionate manner. But it is worth a try. The editors and participants in this volume are to be commended for numerous suggestions and examples which may serve as road markers to that end.

Thirty years ago Dorothy and I sat through a sermon series preached, as we were encouraged to believe, from the book of Acts. The visiting minister selected sections of Acts for each sermon. He read various parts of the text and proceeded to ignore both the whole and the subtexts. For amplification he trumpeted his favorite religious ideas, lambasted those who held the opposite, and interspersed incidents relating to his farm which he visited a few hours every morning. It was not clear what any of this had to do with the Acts texts. Dorothy and I increasingly despaired over sitting through these sessions when we had so many things to do. We were dismayed on the last night when an elder announced that it had been a long time since he had heard such biblical preaching.

As Fleer and Bland indicate in their introductory essay, it is not easy to pinpoint the exact contours of biblical preaching. A case might be made that biblical preaching is narrative preaching. Samuel's sermon was a "declaring of all the saving deeds of the Lord that he performed for you and for your ancestors" (1 Samuel 12:6-18) with applications for the immediate context. Ezra proceeded in the same fashion as he challenged the citizens of Jerusalem to take up their faith once again following the exile (Nehemiah 9:6-37). Stephen, as he spoke before the council, modeled his discourse according to this age old tried and trusted formula (Acts 7:1-53), as did Paul in the synagogue at Antioch of Pisidia (Acts 13:16-41). Peter set out in the same narrative style as he stood before the hushed household of Cornelius, except that "saving deeds" in his sermon were the words and works of Jesus of Nazareth. The other sermons we come upon in Acts are identical in genre. Perhaps we cannot do better than telling the stories about the mighty actions of God.

But there are other approaches in Scripture. Athenians knew neither the stories of Yahweh, nor of his Son. So standing on the Areopagus, Paul commenced with a speech about the universal fear of the deities. He ended announcing Jesus as judge, and his resurrection as the guarantee (Acts 17:22-32). Jesus himself employed an Isaiah text as a profound explication of his identity and ministry (Luke 4:16-28). In the Sermon on the Mount he drew heavily upon Deuteronomy, not so much text after text in sequence, but in order to establish the proper interpretation of various demands of God (Matthew 5:3-7:27). Sometimes texts were brought into topics, for example, by Paul as he discussed the fate of his own people, Israel. He drew from the Torah and the prophets. biblical preaching is not limited to one mode. But always in Scripture the focus is upon the God who revealed himself, and the human response. God acted. He expected his people to react.

I am honored to commend this volume because the editors, David Fleer and Dave Bland are esteemed former students. Furthermore Dave Bland's father, Bob Bland, was a fellow entering student and friend at Harding University in the Fall of 1947. I am also privileged to have had John York and Tim Kelley in class.

I close with this story from Elie Wiesel.

"Invited by a disciple from a neighboring village to attend a circumcision ceremony, a rabbi hires the only coach in the village to take him there. He and the coachman begin the journey in high spirits: the rabbi because he is about to perform a mitzvah, a good deed, and the coachman because he will earn a few zlotys. At the bottom of the first hill the horse halts, exhausted. The coachman dismounts and begins to push the carriage. Of course the rabbi, too, leaves the carriage and helps push. They push and push until they finally arrive at the Hasid's doorstep. That is when the rabbi tells the coachman: "There is something I don't understand. I understand why I am here; the Hasid wishes me to participate in his ceremony. I also understand why you are here; this is how you make your living. But the horse, this poor horse, why did we bring it along?"

Sometimes when the preacher is through, we wonder why he brought along the Scripture. Hopefully, this book will contribute to eliciting a manner of preaching such that those in the pews will no longer wonder what the Scripture, ensconced in the sermon, has to do with their walk with God.

Thomas H. Olbricht
Distinguished Emeritus Professor of Religion,
Pepperdine University

Introduction

An important identity we hold to in the Restoration movement focuses on the roll assigned to Scripture in the task of preaching. We are committed to maintaining the centrality of the Bible in the pulpit. However, Scripture's centrality in the pulpit has recently been challenged.[1] As a result some important questions must be raised: What role did Scripture play in the preaching of the early church? Did the early church preach from specific texts or did they proclaim the incarnate Word? Do we proclaim a book or do we proclaim a person, Jesus Christ?

Preaching is a theological enterprise. But frequently it is reduced to nothing more than preaching from isolated passages. These isolated texts easily end up becoming nothing more than proof-texting on a grandiose scale.

Focus on the Bible can lead to losing sight of the incarnate Word of God, Jesus Christ. In the early church preaching focused on the person of Christ: "For I decided to know nothing among you except Jesus Christ and him crucified" (1 Cor. 2:2). Tom Olbricht observes, "…we are to proclaim the living Lord, not a book for its own sake."[2] In fact, Jesus reprimanded the Jews on one occasion because they searched within the Scriptures to find eternal life. But it would not be found there. Eternal life comes from Jesus Christ (John 5:39-40).

So what do we do with the Bible in preaching? What do we do with texts of Scripture? While it is true that we preach the Gospel–the story of Jesus Christ and him crucified–what is it

---

[1]To this end, David Buttrick offers the following perspective: "Is the whole Bible a book that must be preached simply because it is the Bible and somebody has labeled it as the Word of God? Do we preach to study particular, peculiar biblical passages, or is preaching a theological endeavor that seeks to make sense of life now in view of God's graciousness in Jesus Christ?" See David Buttrick, *A Captive Voice: The Liberation of Preaching* (Louisville: Westminster/John Knox Press, 1994), 11.

[2]Tom Olbricht, "Preaching the Word," *Leaven* (1997) : 36-37. Olbricht traces his personal journey of what it means to preach the word of God which first began with sermons filled with Scripture quoting, then moved to preaching specific texts and finally to preaching Christ.

that makes up this Gospel? Standing behind the Gospel are smaller sometimes odd stories and incidents, that give the Gospel its diversity, force and dynamic. These small quaint texts are the resources for proclaiming the Gospel. Preaching that has no base in specific texts, quickly deteriorates into nothing more than a concern with passing out warm fuzzies on Sunday morning.

Scripture serves as the primary deposit for understanding Gospel. It is the seedbed out of which the Gospel story grows. Early Christian preaching often flowed from specific texts. True, it was not the only way they preached. But they did use specific texts. This was the practice of preaching in the synagogue. When Jesus entered the synagogue in Nazareth to preach, he opened Scripture and read from a specific text in Isaiah (61:1-2; 58:6). From that text, he proclaimed its prophetic fulfillment. In the synagogue, such reading of Scripture followed by instruction of the text was the accepted practice of the day.

Paul implies that specific texts of Scripture were the basis of early Christian preaching. He exhorts Timothy to give attention to the public reading of Scripture, to preaching and teaching (1 Timothy 4:13). For the church to regularly incorporate the reading of Scripture in the public worship assumes that specific texts of Scripture occupied a central role. Paul speaks of the reading of Scripture in the context of preaching and teaching. All three responsibilities are closely tied together. His mandate appears as a standard, not just for Timothy but for what Paul sees as the ideal model to follow.

Preaching specific texts was a dominant practice in the life and identity of the early church. Again, that was by no means the only way in which the early church preached. In Hebrews there is an overarching theological component to the sermon, but still there is lengthy development of specific texts from the Psalter. David Bartlett, who teaches at Yale University Divinity School, reaches the following conclusion in his book on biblical preaching: *"We hold fast the centrality of the text. Of course it is not the Bible we preach but God in Christ. Yet the safest–and most daring–way to discern and proclaim God in Christ is to see* and proclaim through the lens of specific biblical texts." [3]

The preacher cannot access the Gospel without first going through Scripture. The preacher preaches through Scripture to identify the Gospel. [4] Thus, the preacher must preach specific texts in order to enter into the world of the Gospel. Those claiming that preachers preach the Gospel and not the Bible have created too sharp a distinction between preaching texts and preaching the Gospel. [5] If the preacher does not take the smaller texts seriously, then the larger story becomes anemic. The smaller compelling stories make up the infrastructure of faith. They are the source for the Gospel. Only when we take seriously the individual parts, can we understand more clearly the message of the Gospel. Bartlett expresses our commitment succinctly, "Though we use the Bible, we do not preach so that people may encounter the Bible, but so that people may encounter Christ." [6] As the words to the well-known hymn proclaim, it is *"beyond the sacred page"* where we ultimately seek the Lord. [7]

This volume proceeds under the assumption that the good

---

[3] David L. Bartlett, *Between the Bible and the Church: New Metaphors for Biblical Preaching* (Nashville: Abingdon Press, 1999), 151. Emphasis is Bartlett's. Bartlett began his book by making the following claim: ". . . to be sure, the prophets preached not texts, but living oracles; and the apostles preached the testimony of the crucified Christ, though it was not yet written down. But I am neither prophet nor apostle, and the words that bear witness to their witness are contained between the covers of my Bible. Preaching lives under the promise that, where the Word is faithfully and carefully interpreted, God still speaks to God's people." 12.

[4] Carol Antablin Miles, " 'Singing the Songs of Zion' and Other Sermons from the Margins of the Canon," *Koinonia 6* (1995) : 154.

[5] See the following two articles by Edward Farley; "Preaching the Bible and Preaching the Gospel," *Theology Today* 51 no 1 (1994) : 90-103; "Toward a New Paradigm for Preaching," in *Preaching As A Theological Task: World, Gospel, Scripture*, Thomas G. Long and Edward Farley, eds. (Louisville: Westminster John Knox Press, 1996), 165-175. Preaching the Gospel rather than texts of Scripture is what Farley advocates. Dividing Scripture into many parts, each with a lesson for life, drains the narrative of its power.

[6] Bartlett, p. 13.

[7] "Break Thou the Bread of Life," words by Mary Artemisia Lathbury, 1877. Unfortunately more recent hymnals edit the words of the hymn to read "within the sacred page I seek thee, Lord." See *Songs of Faith and Praise*, compiled and edited by Alton H. Howard (West Monroe, LA: Howard Publishing Co, 1994).

news of the Gospel flows out of Scripture. As editors we are committed to proclaiming that Gospel through responsible use of biblical texts.

Responsible preaching of texts occurs when the best of biblical scholarship is wedded to a faith in God and a commitment to his church. The purpose of this volume on Luke/Acts is to call on biblical scholarship to inform the content of preaching. We challenge preaching to root itself in Scripture and depend on the Holy Spirit for proclamation. Through such a marriage, preaching fulfills its task of shaping God's people into a mature body of Christ. The contributors to this volume all share a deep commitment to such a goal.

This book had its inception in a Sermon Seminar conducted at Rochester College in Rochester, Michigan, May of 1999. On that occasion, a gathering of preachers assembled to listen to and dialogue about the task of preaching from Luke/Acts. Out of that interactive climate, this volume proceeded.

Our intention is to combine the best of academia with the best of practical ministry. The contributors were chosen for their involvement in both the world of scholarship as well as the life of the church. We are not interested in engaging in abstract theological excursions. Nor are we interested in a "how to" manual on preaching. Rather we want to equip preachers to reflect seriously about the task of preaching. Specifically, we want to challenge preachers to think responsibly about preaching from Luke/Acts.

Part I addresses homiletical issues and theological themes that influence the way one preaches Luke/Acts. We begin with an opening chapter on preaching. The chapter deals with a current tension in homiletical theory that directly affects pulpit practice and shapes the identity of God's church.

The four chapters that follow focus on various aspects of the Luke/Acts narrative. In chapter two Tom Long explores the possibilities for preaching the pronouncement stories in the Gospel of Luke. Tim Kelley surveys the landscape regarding Luke's perspective on wealth with an eye on implications for the pulpit. Greg Sterling explores the theme of prayer in Luke/Acts. Dean Smith follows up on Sterling's chapter by offering suggestions for developing sermons on prayer.

Part II comprises a series of sermons from Luke/Acts.

Chapter six contains six sermons on Luke by John York. The seventh chapter includes six sermons on Acts by David Fleer. Each sermon in these chapters was preached in a local church or church related setting. We hope these twelve sermons will trigger ideas for how texts in Luke and Acts might be preached. Our intention is not for the preacher to imitate or copy these sermons in the pulpit. Such practice would demonstrate poor preaching. One has to communicate God's word differently to different audiences. Rather, the sermons are intended to generate thought about how to preach particular passages. The sermons attempt to flesh out theories, themes and ideas developed in earlier chapters.

The context for this book is rooted in the life of the local church. We desire to integrate biblical scholarship and homiletical theory with the task of preaching Luke/Acts. Our prayer is that the responsible integration of these resources will increase the ability of the Holy Spirit to empower preachers for faithful proclamation of God's word. To that end we give God the glory.

David Fleer
Dave Bland

Part I

The Task of Preaching Luke/Acts

Chapter One:
Tension In Preaching

DAVID FLEER AND DAVE BLAND

Tensions persist in preaching today. Preacher and congregation feel these tensions every Sunday morning when the minister lays out notes, opens the Bible, and announces the sermon's text. One tension remains fixed in the mind of the preacher and in the hearts of the listeners. The preacher's desire for sermons to faithfully reflect the message of biblical texts stands at odds with the congregation's pleas for self-help homilies that address her most pressing personal problems. Another tension resides in the audience feeling the need to hear sermons that reflect the "old paths" which strain the preacher's understanding of what the "good news" really entails. Even within the reflective preacher's mind, the conflict between what the Bible appears to say and what the meaning is for the congregation creates a holy tremble for this one who claims to speak for God. The strain not only pulls preacher from congregation but creates tension among competing camps within the church. These tensions are maintained, in part, by our understanding of how the Bible is supposed to function in the sermon.

One of us recently experienced this tension while listening to a sermon developed from 1 Samuel 17, David's battle with Goliath. The preacher paraphrased the story raising historical/textual questions (just when did Goliath die?), narrative curiosities (why five stones? how large were the stones? how fast were they slung?), and psychological insights (what was Saul thinking as he watched David? Who are the Goliaths in our lives?). The preacher developed the sermon in quite an interesting manner. But, the sermon ignored the movements and emphases of the text. For example, when noting the battlefield dialogue of David and Goliath, the preacher concluded, "David 'one-upped' Goliath."

As the preacher moved on to other historical developments and cultural observations, I stayed with Samuel, reading closely the language of David. What I noticed was not so much the verbal superiority of David but his covenantal language. Not only was Goliath an "uncircumcised Philistine" but the Lord would prevail against all apparent odds. God talk is in every line that David utters.[1] These details should have cast the sermon in an entirely different direction and should have superseded the psychological bent of the sermon's application. The biblical text before me was more interesting and held more promise for matters of import than the sermon.

This instance of sermon-created tension grew out of differing expectations for the sermon. I came to the service desiring challenge or uplift. I received neither. I wanted to be reminded of the reality of God through a strong prophetic word. I received instead "trivial facts" and psychological insights. Any preacher who dares to conduct an exit interview with frustrated members hears and feels this tension. Whether the disgruntled church member leaves for more relevant climes or transfers to a congregation where he or she can hear "the Truth," at the heart of the matter is the role of the Bible in preaching.

The crisis is not new. In the Restoration Movement we have long thrived on the injunction to preach from the Bible to the needs of the church and society. We have long desired that our preaching be faithful to Scripture. Yet, we have consistently wrestled between the ideals of "good news or old paths," or "personal needs or living in the text." We have struggled with the place of the Bible in the pulpit. Consider two approaches to preaching that have characterized our movement.

Concordance and Expository Preaching
Early in the Restoration Movement "concordance preaching"[2] dominated the way in which Scripture was used in the sermon. Verses of Scripture were viewed as pieces of a

---

[1]Consider the number of references to God and YHWH in 1 Samuel 17: 26, 36f, 45, 46, 47.

[2]Leonard Allen uses this phrase in a manner similar to our definition. C. Leonard Allen, *The Cruciform Church: Becoming a Cross-Shaped People in a Secular World* (Abilene, TX: ACU Press, 1990), 40-41.

puzzle the preacher put together in a correct pattern around a specific subject such as baptism or repentance. The sermon became a litany of verses quoted from all over the pages of Scripture. The preacher, functioning each Sunday like a systematic theologian, reached the pinnacle of his homiletic skills when Scripture quotations were uninterrupted by commentary. J. W. McGarvey even pronounced, "When preaching thus, we are preaching the Word."[3] This style of preaching, while popularized within the Restoration Movement through Alexander Campbell and other pioneer preachers, continues through some Schools of Preaching and remains a staple in other Evangelical traditions.

The concordance sermon, however, has met with some criticism. For example, such sermons can become nothing more than a catalogue of rational arguments and appeals.[4] The content of the concordance sermon also serves as a way for some preachers to disguise their own theological orientation (or bias) through a Scripture-quoting mosaic.[5] Today, many auditors claim that they can identify a preacher's School of Preaching background from the theology embedded in his sermons.[6] David Bartlett summarized this "honorable tradition" of preaching as one which "overwhelms and under illumines the mind."[7] Indeed, who among us has the theological skills to

---

[3]Cited in Michael W. Casey, *Saddlebags, City Streets, and Cyberspace: A History of Preaching in the Churches of Christ*, (Abilene, TX: ACU Press, 1995), 32.

[4]Such are the results of Alexander Campbell's "scientific" approach to biblical studies and preaching. For further development, see Casey, *Saddlebags*, 25-36 and Allen, *Cruciform Church*, 19-41.

[5]Of course, any style of preaching can be used in an attempt to disguise one's theological orientation. Concordance preaching's chief liability resides in its disregard for the theological and literary context of the quoted text.

[6]Appropriately, church historian Richard Hughes categorizes Schools of Preaching by their theological orientation. Thus, Sunset's emphasis on grace dominates the preaching heard from its ex -students. Richard T. Hughes, *Reviving the Ancient Faith: The Story of Churches of Christ in America*, (Grand Rapids: Eerdmans, 1996), 330-333.

[7]David L. Bartlett, *Between the Bible and the Church: New Metaphors for Biblical Preaching* (Nashville: Abingdon Press, 1999), 22-23. Fred Craddock is much harsher in his judgment of "thoughtless, concordance preaching of those whose sermons are little more than accumulations of unrelated verses." See Fred Craddock, *Preaching* (Nashville: Abingdon Press,1985), 159.

follow the contours of such a journey through texts?

Another approach popularly labeled "expository preaching" has thrived throughout the twentieth century. While the meaning of the term varies among its exponents,[8] the characteristic understanding of an expository sermon gravitates around its focus on a specific unit of biblical text in context, often ending with application. At the heart of this didactic approach lies the commitment to unpack the meaning of a particular text in its literary and historical context.[9] The result of such a commitment often leads preachers to devote a significant portion of the sermon to sharing important background information on historical events or cultural customs that shed light on a darkened text.

A generation ago Harry Emerson Fosdick led the attack against expository sermons with the memorable observation, "Only the preacher proceeds still upon the idea that folk come to church desperately anxious to discover what happened to the Jebusites."[10] We might add, "…or to know the speed of David's rock." Again, at issue is the tension between the preacher's understanding of what it means to be faithful to Scripture and the desire to address the felt needs of the audience. Fosdick criticized expository preaching because he saw it as irrelevant to the needs of contemporary hearers.

In our conversations with preachers who advocate preaching expository sermons, we have detected another problem. When

---

[8]Advocates of expository preaching have complicated its definition by creating distinctions in sermon types in terms of the length of the passage being exposited or in terms of the location of the text in the sermon's outline. Dependent on Andrew Blackwood's nomenclature, a "topical" sermon focuses on a key word, phrase, or idea in the text. A "textual" sermon flows out of one or two verses from scripture. "Expository" sermons develop from texts longer than two or three verses. See Andrew W. Blackwood, *Preaching From the Bible* (NY: Abingdon-Cokesbury Press, 1941), 38. Also see Blackwood's *Expository Preaching for Today: Case Studies of Bible Passages* (New York: Abingdon-Cokesbury Press, 1953),13. To add to the confusion, many current preachers were trained under the theory of Charles Koller where expository sermons were defined by the presence of points and sub-points originating in the biblical text. Various techniques for developing these points were the focus of some homiletic literature. See Charles Koller, *Expository Preaching Without Notes* (Grand Rapids: Baker Book House, 1962). For a contemporary development of Koller see Donald L. Hamilton, Homiletical Handbook (Nashville: Broadman, 1992).

[9]See Sidney Greidanus, *The Modern Preacher and the Ancient Text: Interpreting and Preaching Biblical Literature* (Grand Rapids: Eerdmans, 1988), 11.

[10]Harry Emerson Fosdick, "What's the Matter with Preaching?" *Harpers Monthly*, 157 (July, 1928): 135.

we question the expressed opinion, "I really like to preach expository sermons," we often hear the preacher reveal the belief that commitment to such a method guarantees preaching's faithfulness to Scripture. The problem, however, is that some of these expository sermons too often consist of little more than "jacking up a text and running a sermon under it."[11] The text simply jump-starts the sermon. Thus, the preacher can defend his theological position on a difficult topic, by hiding behind the text: "This isn't me preaching, this is the Word of God!" The deceptive beauty is that this style of preaching appears to give authority to the preacher.

In the Restoration movement, our commitment to the Bible has resulted in a struggle to know the place of Scripture in the sermon. How does the sermon faithfully use Scripture? Is it through concordance preaching or expository preaching or some other way? How do preachers faithfully use Scripture to speak to the needs of people today?

Seeker Targeted[12] Sermons

While preachers wrestle with their faithfulness to Scripture, congregations become more vocal in their desire to hear practical lessons from the pulpit. There are growing numbers within our congregations who passionately call for the church's programs and the preacher's sermons to speak directly to community needs. They demand, "We must address issues moms and dads want to hear, provide classes for their children, and advertise the event with a catchy sermon title. Then, we'll persuade the community to come to our church." Family members and friends will attend, they promise, if "lessons" are designed to meet people right where they live in today's complex and confusing world.

The congregation's request actually imitates the practical life skills found in the appealing and popular format of the

---

[11]C. Michael Moss, "The Exposition of Scripture," in Man of God: Essays of the Life and Work of the Preacher (Nashville: Gospel Advocate Co., 1996), 213.

[12]Charles Arn distinguishes between "seeker-sensitive services" and "seeker-targeted services." The first term describes a worship that assumes those in attendance are predominantly Christians. The second term describes a worship that assumes those in attendance are predominantly non-Christians. See Charles Arn, How To Start A New Service: Your Church Can Reach New People (Grand Rapids: Baker Books, 1997), 100. Thanks to Chris Altrock for pointing us to this resource.

Application Bibles. With their Bible's colored boxes, fore-grounding quick lessons for improving everything from one's sexual needs to career enhancement, Christians grow accustomed, from their own Bibles (!), to locating life lessons before even reading the text.

Congregational demands find academic support from outside the field of biblical studies. There, sermon evaluation originates from a vantage that differs from the realm of the text. For example, sociologist William Martin, in his fine overview of American revivalists, judges, "There is nothing mysterious about Moody's success. His theology, style, and technique were perfectly suited to his age."[13] Billy Sunday's career ended with "marked suddenness" when "he lost his grip on the national consciousness."[14] Martin further assesses the strengths and weaknesses of American revivalists through Billy Graham by this sociological standard: the sermon's success in matching the desires of the audience. One expects this from a sociological vantage. But, we are not sociologists, nor are we psychologists, cultural analysts, or micro economists. We are preachers of the Gospel of Jesus Christ. Martin and other social scientists aptly describe one part of the tension. They fail, however, to reveal the entire picture and the cause for the strain. The result of all this leads to some preachers embracing the social scientist's myopic perspective and becoming audience driven as they formulate their message.

So we continue to face the reality of a tension between "gospel preaching" and "culturally sensitive" preaching. Our struggle, however, remains but a microcosm of the larger war[15] waging in the Protestant Christian world. Consider, for example, the findings of USC researcher Donald Miller and his work with Southern California-rooted churches, principally

---

[13] William Martin, *A Prophet With Honor: The Billy Graham Story* (NY: William Morrow and Company, Inc., 1991), 46. Moody's style, Martin assesses, "fit the taste of the times," 47.

[14] Martin, 52.

[15] Marva Dawn aptly uses the term "worship wars" to describe the polarization in Mainline Protestant congregations struggling between traditional and contemporary forms of worship. Marva Dawn, *Reaching Out Without Dumbing Down: A Theology of Worship for the Turn-of-the-Century Culture* (Grand Rapids: Eerdmans, 1995).

those associated with Calvary Chapel, Hope Chapel and Vineyard Christian Fellowship. Miller argues that the current transformation within Christianity is not about doctrine, but the medium of Christianity. That is, "new paradigm churches" have discarded traditional habits of Protestant Christianity and appropriated contemporary cultural forms including church polity, worship and preaching.[16]

We can further delineate the new reality with the question, whose world counts? For many growing churches, the answer rings clear: the seeker. When an unchurched person walks through the church door, he or she asks, "Are you up to date and contemporary, or locked in antiquity?"[17] In this new setting where the church building is purposely made to appear similar to corporate headquarters, or a state-of-the-art theater, the kind of preaching demanded by the contemporary listener "both identifies and aids the listener in solving the problems and crises that plague his or her life. It is the contemporary world that counts."[18] Churches find themselves shaping the worship, the preaching, the ministries of the church, and even the physical plant with the primary intention of attracting the seeker.

Listening congregations, preachers come to discover, express little interest in receiving a volley of isolated scripture quotations, nor in hearing detailed comments on large blocks of text, nor in rehearsing cultural nuances of ancient societies. Congregations demand life-related preaching which, they surmise, must be easy to obtain from the Bible. How are we to work through this apparent impasse?

The New Homiletic
About the same time individuals began to demand

---

[16]In these churches, the informal sermons focus primarily on explaining texts of Scripture. These churches are, in the words of Miller, "the harbingers of postdenominational Christianity." The "postdenominational" Christian world that Miller describes has been, for some time, labeled as Mainline or Evangelical. The old denominational monikers of Baptist, Presbyterian, or Lutheran no longer remain accurate or useful. Donald E. Miller, "The Reinvented Church: Styles and Strategies," *The Christian Century*, 116 (December 22-29, 1999): 1250.

[17]Lucy Lind Hogan, "Rethinking Context: The Significance of Hermeneutical Starting Points," (Papers of the Annual Meeting for the Academy of Homiletics, December 2-4, 1999, Denver), 138.

[18]Hogan, "Rethinking Context," 138.

"need-meeting sermons," a new way of treating the biblical text appeared in the field of homiletics. In an effort to connect with contemporary audiences, focus changed from explaining the text to experiencing the text. The catalyst for this shift occurred with the 1971 publication of Fred Craddock's *As One Without Authority*. Craddock called for an engagement of preacher, congregation, and biblical text so that listeners could experience "the word of God." He claimed, "Sermons should proceed or move in such a way as to give the listener something to think, feel, decide, and do during the preaching."[19] In recommending the active participation of the listener, Craddock suggested preachers craft sermons that enable the co-creation of understanding. Craddock explained, "Is not the real event in preaching the creation of new meaning at the point of intersection between text and listener, rather than in the carting of information from one to the other?"[20] To this end sermons are composed to allow the congregation to experience the preacher's own process of hermeneutical insight.[21] Moving away from a deductive model of presentation, Craddock's means of engaging listeners in the active pursuit of the effect of the biblical text required an inductive presentation.[22]

Craddock's seminal work launched a creative and stimulating line of homiletic thought, appropriately termed "the new homiletic."[23] Like Craddock, other theorists and practitioners began to advocate preaching sermons that reached

---

[19]Craddock, *Preaching*, 25.

[20]Craddock, *Preaching*, 148.

[21]Craddock clarifies that a good sermon is the result of two "eurekas." The minister has an "aha!" experience in the exegetical work and then another "aha!" when locating an appropriate sermonic form. Thus, "The process of arriving at something to say is to be distinguished from the process of determining how to say it." Craddock, *Preaching*, 84.

[22]Fred Craddock, *As One Without Authority: Essays on Inductive Preaching* (Nashville: Abingdon, 1971), 157.

[23]While Craddock is often identified as the source of the "New Homiletic," the phrase seems to have first been coined by David Randolph. See David James Randolph, *The Renewal of Preaching* (Philadelphia: Fortress Press, 1969) : vii. Randolph observes, "The genius of preaching, as it is here understood, is its eventfulness. What is crucial for homiletics is not so much what the sermon 'is'but what the sermon 'does'" (17). Thanks to Bob Reid for identifying this source for us.

the listeners through imagination rather than by reason.[24] At the same time, the new homiletic developed a variety of emphases. For example, Eugene Lowry became an advocate of the narrative sermon, which adhered to the sequential plot form: conflict, complication, sudden shift and unfolding.[25] In another direction, Thomas G. Long voiced concern for the literary form of the biblical text and urged preachers to regenerate the impact of a text so that the word of God can be active in a new setting.[26]

Many preachers find narrative preaching and other forms of the new homiletic engaging and effective. Like the interest in expository preaching, much in narrative preaching commends itself. Consider the following experience to be representative of the power of this type of preaching.

Nearly a decade ago one of us preached a sermon from Luke 11:1-13, the Lord's Prayer.[27] The sermon was a didactic effort to justify personal and congregational use of the words in Luke 11:1-4. Recently, we happened upon another sermon from the same biblical text, this one crafted by Fred Craddock. The contrast between the two sermons highlights the direction the new homiletic takes. On the one hand, my sermon offered instruction on the Lord's Prayer. Craddock's sermon, on the other hand, effectively encourages the auditor to *do* the Lord's Prayer. After hearing Craddock's, "Lord Teach Us to Pray,"[28] listeners find themselves enraptured by the vivid images and pictures of the sermon. Even more captivating, listeners come away from the sermon eager to engage in prayer, to do precisely what the biblical text wishes readers to do! Listeners

---

[24]For a more detailed overview, see Robert Reid, Jeffery Bullock, and David Fleer, "Preaching As the Creation of an Experience: The Not-So-Rational Revolution of the New Homiletic," *The Journal of Communication and Religion*, 18 (March, 1995): 1-9.

[25]Eugene L. Lowry, *The Sermon: Dancing the Edge of Mystery* (Nashville: Abingdon, 1997). For Lowry, "plot" takes precedence over the more general, and generally misunderstood, "narrative."

[26]Thomas G. Long, *Preaching and the Literary Forms of the Bible* (Philadelphia: Fortress, 1989), 33-34.

[27]David Fleer, "Let Us Pray the Lord's Prayer," *Restoration Quarterly*, 32 (Third Quarter 1990): 179-185.

[28]Fred B. Craddock, "Lord, Teach Us to Pray," in Ronald J. Allen, *Patterns of Preaching: A Sermon Sampler*, (St. Louis: Chalice Press, 1998), 31-35.

desire to pray during the life experiences of joy or quarreling or success or failure–just as Craddock rehearsed in the sermon and just as Luke rehearsed in the biblical text. This is the common trait of Craddock's work: filling the sermon with subtle and rhetorical invitations to enact the biblical text. Indeed, there remains much in narrative preaching to commend it.

Just now, however, the new homiletic, particularly narrative preaching, is coming under some heavy fire. One critique comes from Charles Campbell whose most formidable problem with narrative preaching lies in the source of the sermon's creation.[29] Narrative preaching begins with the understood needs of the people, that is, their situation or experience in life. The problem is that not all expressed desires reflect the intention or meaning of Scripture. More to the point: human experiences are not the common bond for a congregation. What ties the church together is not family, job, or self-related concerns. What hearers share in common, claims Campbell, is baptism and Scripture. For Campbell and other postliberals,[30] the world of the Bible is the Real World.

For a model of preaching, Campbell looks to Walter Brueggemann who rather than encouraging listeners to find their stories in Scripture, suggests that the biblical story describes the hearer's story. This shift is subtle but significant. Campbell and Brueggemann desire for the listener to be co-opted by the biblical story and not use Scripture for one's own devices.[31]

A second criticism of narrative preaching resides in the fact that it improperly shifts the focus of the Bible from character to plot. Narrative preaching, so often enamored by the form of

---

[29]Charles L. Campbell, *Preaching Jesus: New Directions for Homiletics in Hans Frei's Post liberal Theology*, (Grand Rapids: Eerdmanns, 1997).

[30]Roger Olson defines the term in this way: Postliberal theology "seeks to base Christian faith on the identity and presence of Jesus Christ in the narrative-shaped community of God's people. The legitimate basis for all Christian reflection is not 'modern culture'or any culture independent of the gospel, but the language and culture of the church created and nurtured by the story of Jesus and his redemptive life, death, and resurrection" (p. 31). See Roger Olson, "Back to the Bible (Almost): Why Yale Postliberal Theologians Deserve an Evangelical Hearing," *Christianity Today* 40 (May 20, 1996): 31-34.

[31]Campbell, 197.

Scripture, misses the subject, Jesus of Nazareth. Instead, the parable becomes the primary interpretive tool for narrative preaching. Following C. H. Dodd's definition, a parable is "a metaphor or simile...arresting the hearer by its vividness or strangeness, and leaving the mind in sufficient doubt about its precise application to tease it into active thought."[32] Campbell explains, "As long as parables remain the central focus for preaching, then plot can remain the primary concern."[33] When one turns to the Bible, argues Campbell and other postliberals, one finds no such concern for style. Rather, the function of the gospels is to render the identity of Jesus of Nazareth.[34]

Campbell's corrective shifts the focus back from parable to gospel and from plot to character by moving from matters of literary form to "the particular ascriptive logic of the gospel stories."[35] He counsels, "If preachers would linger with the identity of Jesus before moving too quickly to his meaningfulness, they might be surprised."[36] After all, the object of our worship is not a particular genre, but the One who is revealed through the literature of the Bible.

Narrative preaching continues to offer some constructive guidance for managing the tension that exists between the preacher's desire to faithfully proclaim the message of Scripture and the audience's demand for self-help sermons. However, the momentum of narrative preaching has frequently carried it more into the world of the listener than into the world of Scripture.

Toward a Solution

The current tension in preaching appears to demand an unpleasant choice. On the one hand, we recognize the dull biblicism that retains the odors and forms of yesterday: dry excursions into foreign cultures and dead languages. On the other hand, we see a model that shows high sensitivity to the visitor's comfort zone and targets sermons to the earthy and

---

[32]C. H. Dodd, *The Parables of the Kingdom* (New York: Charles Scribner's Sons, 1961), 5.

[33]Campbell, 190.

[34]See especially Campbell, 189-220.

[35]Campbell, 200.

[36]Campbell, 201.

specific needs of "unchurched Harry." We already know the limitations of resuscitating concordance or exegetical preaching. At the same time, we have little regard for sermons primarily created from sociological analysis. We do not seek to repackage the popular evangelical homiletic within our own peculiar worship setting: sermons that target seekers in a Church of Christ environment.

What alternatives, then, do preachers have? One viable option arises from the postliberal effort to invite listeners into the real world of Scripture. The post liberal homiletic seeks to reverse the flow of traffic on the hermeneutical bridge between Scripture and culture. The popular and dominant theory post liberals seek to correct moves traffic across the bridge by dragging the biblical text into the world of contemporary culture. Post liberals, however, wish to reverse the flow of traffic by leading the contemporary culture into the world of Scripture.

Astrong impetus for the post liberal view comes from Gail O'Day who claims Scripture itself presents a postliberal perspective.[37] O'Day uses sermons in Deuteronomy as an example of the direction the traffic flows. According to O'Day, the bulk of Deuteronomy was written sometime during the eighth century and was used as the basis for Josiah's reforms. Thus, Deuteronomy was not initially addressed to the people of Israel about to cross over into the Promised Land. Rather, it was written to people who had long lived in the land. As such, the sermons in Deuteronomy invite the pre-exilic and exilic audiences to imagine themselves on the plains of Moab listening to the speeches of Moses before embarking on the conquest of Canaan.

Through the sermons of Deuteronomy, the exilic audience relives the wilderness experience of an earlier Israelite generation. The sermons incorporate people into the world view of the Israelites on the plains of Moab. Deuteronomy represents the old traditions to the people of the eighth century.[38] The story

---

[37] Gail R. O'Day, "Bible and Sermon: The Conversation Between Text and Preacher," in *Sharing Heaven's Music*, Barry L. Callen, ed. (Nashville: Abingdon Press, 1995) : 69-81.

[38] The eighth century audience even engages in a recital of the exodus events as though they were there (see Deuteronomy 26:5-11): "When the Egyptians treated us harshly and afflicted us...and he brought us into this place and gave us this land" (vv. 6-9).

and traditions of the distant past become the present generation's story. The sermons take the traditions and imaginatively fuse the present generation into that world. Based on the model of Deuteronomy, O'Day concludes, "The challenge for the preacher is to open up this conversation in his or her own preaching so that…[present day audiences] can imagine their lives transformed and renewed by the possibilities of the biblical texts."[39]

O'Day's proposal flows out of the postliberal perspective and her paradigm for preaching aligns with the theology of George Lindbeck. The attraction and overwhelming challenge of their claim is that the real world is the one depicted in the Bible. Lindbeck claimed, "…it is the religion instantiated in scripture which defines being, truth, goodness, and beauty, and the nonscriptural exemplifications of these realities need to be transformed into figures…of the scriptural ones."[40]

We realize the truthfulness of the postliberal claim in its hedge against the overwhelming tide of popular culture. From the pulpit we sometimes sense that the preacher has lifted an article from *Reader's Digest*, infused it with a handful of sound bites from the pages of the Bible and preached it as the Word of God. Nearly two decades ago Lindbeck warned against this type of appropriation. He argued that when churches "embrace in one fashion or another the majority of the population [they] must cater willy-nilly to majority trends."[41] Once churches have succumbed to the movement of society, Lindbeck further warned, it is "difficult for [churches] to attract assiduous catachumens even among their own children, and when they do, they generally prove wholly incapable of providing effective instruction in distinctly Christian language and practice."[42] In the midst of these currents, the postliberals advise, "[preaching]…should therefore resist the clamor of the

---

[39]O'Day, 81.

[40]George A. Lindbeck, The Nature of Doctrine: Religion and Theology in a Postliberal Age (Philadelphia: Westminster Press, 1984), 118.

[41]Lindbeck, *Nature of Doctrine*, 133.

[42]ibid.

religiously interested public for what is currently fashionable and immediately intelligible." [43]

What we find admirable about O'Day's and Lindbeck's theological perspective is their high view of Scripture. The biblical text remains the center of gravity for the task of preaching. The contemporary world is interpreted, critiqued, and judged in light of the world of Scripture. Twenty-first century cultures are held accountable to the gravitational forces of the biblical world.

Yet, the postliberal argument that life in Scripture is the location for real living can be read as a limited enterprise which treats audiences as one whether they be ancient Jerusalem or Athens or modern Detroit or Memphis. The gravitational forces of the biblical world disregard specific contexts and cultures of our present lives. In short, our concern with postliberal preaching is that it does not adequately engage the audience. It evades the evidence from the exit interviews of former members and ignores what lies beneath the gushing testimonies of those attending the growing community churches: folk long to be engaged by preaching.

The problem accelerates when listeners have little or no familiarity with the biblical stories and traditions. How can preachers invite an audience into a world about which the audience knows nothing? It is difficult, perhaps impossible, to be incorporated into a world to which one cannot relate. When the biblical world is totally foreign to the audience, what can motivate these listeners to plunge into this other world?

Furthermore, we are not convinced that the traffic on the hermeneutical bridge must be unidirectional. On the one hand, we do not simply absorb people into the world of Scripture. On the other hand, neither do we desire to absorb Scripture into culture. While inviting hearers to share the world of Scripture, preachers also have responsibility to locate points of connection with contemporary culture so those hearers better understand their real needs and responsibilities.

Christ entered the human world at a specific point in time. He identified intimately with the culture of his day in order to lead people to his Father. "The Word became flesh and dwelt

---

[43]ibid., 134.

among us." God continues to penetrate the world with his word through preaching. Throughout Scripture God called prophets and preachers to contextualize their message in ever changing circumstances. These messengers of God did more than just read texts to the new audiences they encountered. They incarnated the word they proclaimed. God placed the treasure of his word, of all things, in earthen vessels. God continues to initiate the move toward us in order to call us into the world of his kingdom. In modeling God's movement, preachers proclaim the Gospel in specific cultural contexts. To call people to the kingdom of God requires that preachers understand and identify with their specific cultural context. In turn, it requires preachers to use concrete images, experiences, stories, and current thought in order to prepare the specific culture to receive the counter story of the biblical text.

We believe that it is possible to be biblical and engage audiences. We sympathize with postliberals who look to Scripture to define meaning. We turn to Scripture, however, not just because it is in the Christian canon but also because Scripture understands our condition better than we. Scripture is capable of asking harder questions than we know how to ask or wish to express. We believe, therefore, that Scripture can effectively be more "practical" than we know or care to be.

We suggest, therefore, that preachers allow Scripture to engage us through the clues it supplies. One means of accomplishing this end is through genre-sensitive preaching where the relationship between the literary forms and content of biblical texts implies differences in how they are heard and preached. A form sensitive approach to preaching claims that a sermon should attempt to accomplish what a particular text accomplishes.[44] Honoring the creative nuances of literary types within Scripture, form sensitive preaching celebrates the power of Scripture to impact listeners by re-presenting the biblical text so that what happened to the original hearers happens now to those who hear it afresh. With Craddock, we wish to *get* to the world *through* the biblical text. In other words, we believe that textual sensitivity will do far more for the needs of listeners than targeting seekers. Out of one's exegetical work comes sermon

---

[44]See Thomas G. Long, *Preaching and the Literary Forms of the Bible*, (Philadelphia: Fortress, 1989).

preparation and even the bridge to the sermon is developed from a close reading of the text.

Consider the opening lines to Craddock's "Lord Teach Us to Pray." He begins, "This is an awkward moment for Jesus and the disciples. They are together–thirteen of them–when one begins to pray. What do you do when one person in a group starts praying? Do you leave? Do you keep one eye open? Do you wish you were somewhere else?"[45] Craddock's sermon launches itself from the difficulty of public prayer and then proceeds to sketch additional vignettes with Craddock himself uncomfortable at saying or hearing prayer in a restaurant: "I'm not opposed to prayer, but, well…in the Pizza Hut?"[46] It is the sermon's starting point but it is not the sermon. The sermon is from Luke 11:1-13 and moves rhetorically into the text and its larger context to capture the essential motivation that may have driven the request of the Twelve and may drive us to desire to pray.

For Craddock, occasionally the contemporary experience puts "flesh on bones." In the above sermon, however, Craddock gives voice to all persons' problems with prayer. Thus, he provides necessary backdrop to the disciples question in Luke 11:2. It is precisely what Luke has done in the gospel, up to 11:1.[47] The heart of Craddock's sermon is encouragement to pray, precisely what Luke has Jesus do with the vignettes in 11:5-13.

The sermon does not begin where exegesis began. However, the preacher has taken strong clues from Luke, created an appropriate image and returned to the text to follow the sharp curves and sudden turns of the biblical story. Here is Craddock's tension, respecting the fine detail of the biblical story and opening wells of emotion and piquing hearers' understanding.

Postliberalism has reminded us of "true north:" that the real world is reflected in the Bible. But preachers cannot treat lightly the world in which the listeners live. Listeners are so

---

[45]Fred B. Craddock, "Lord, Teach Us to Pray," in Ronald J. Allen, *Patterns of Preaching: A Sermon Sampler*, (St. Louis: Chalice Press, 1998) ,31.

[46]Craddock, "Lord, Teach Us to Pray," 31.

[47]See Greg Sterling's chapter in this volume,. 58f.

absorbed in the language and values of their secular culture that the preacher must penetrate and understand that world before presenting a counter world. Listeners need guidance in changing their worldview. Simply thrusting the biblical world alongside the contemporary world, then calling listeners to the former does not empower listeners to assimilate their own world into the biblical world. They must be given ways to identify with the biblical world that relate to their specific and unique cultural context. Engaging the audience with the biblical text the sermon proclaims *is* a part of the real world. Therefore we are disinclined to dismiss Long and Craddock among the New Homiliticans, knowing that the taproot of their theory of preaching is the biblical text and that their goal is to speak to the deepest level of human need.

In his popular history of preaching in the Churches of Christ, Michael Casey observes, "One of the hallmarks of preaching in the Churches of Christ is the insistence that it be biblical. The problem is that the definition of the term 'biblical' varies widely."[48] By tracing the historical development of the traditions of preaching in this branch of the Restoration Movement, Casey demonstrates that preaching has always adapted to cultural influences. What is needed, he claims, "is preaching that is faithful to the gospel regardless of the cultural form preaching takes."[49] In this volume and the volumes that follow, we hope to put flesh on the idea of preaching that is faithful to the gospel. The challenge we wish to set before preachers in this current volume is to so honor the text and the One whom it venerates that we communicate the riches of Scripture believing that it reveals God's response to the human condition.

---

[48]Casey, *Saddlebags*, x-xi.

[49]Casey, *Saddlebags*, ix.

Chapter Two:
Preaching the Pronouncement Stories in Luke

THOMAS G. LONG

Diderot called it "l'esprit de l'escalier" ("the wit of the staircase"), the common human experience of thinking of something witty or wise you could have said, some choice riposte, too late, only as you are climbing the staircase to bed after the party. The underlying idea, of course, is that human exchanges often have moments of opportunity, brief windows of time when just the right word will bring mirth or understanding or triumph. But such moments have brief half-lives; the window closes, the opportunity dissipates, and we are left climbing the staircase, slapping our forehead, and wishing we had thought to say that then.

Of the many things the early church remembered about Jesus, apparently one is that he rarely if ever suffered from the wit of the staircase. The church told of a Jesus who, in times of conversation, debate, and interrogation, was consistently able to seize the moment and to speak just the right word at precisely the right moment to achieve exactly the right result. Indeed, a number of these conversational lightning strikes are preserved in the Gospels as stories that have the goal of showcasing a wise or witty or provocative statement of Jesus. Bultmann, in The History of the Synoptic Tradition, termed these literary forms "apopthogems,"[1] but a phrase coined much earlier by Vincent Taylor–pronouncement stories[2]–is most commonly used today.

---

[1]Rudolf Bultmann, *The History of the Synoptic Tradition*, Revised Edition (New York: Harper and Row, 1968), 11-69.

[2]Vincent Taylor, *The Formation of the Gospel Tradition* (London: Macmillan, 1933), 29-30, 63-87.

How Are Pronouncement Stories Built?

New Testament pronouncement stories, to risk tautology, are simply delivery vehicles for pronouncements, for pithy statements of Jesus. That much is obvious. As such, though, they are the kind of biblical texts that can make preachers cranky. What, after all, is there to preach in a pronouncement story? One could repeat the pronouncement, I suppose, and attempt to draw lessons for today, but that would be a narrow ledge on which to stand. True, pronouncement stories are narratives, often a preacher's dream, but pronouncement narratives often lack the rich story lines and interesting characters so homiletically fruitful in other biblical tales. Pronouncement stories appear to be structured more like jokes–narrative setups in the service of punch lines–or like fortune cookies–narrative pastry wrapped around epigrams. However, when we look more closely at the structure of the typical pronouncement story, the form becomes more intricate, more rhetorically interesting, and perhaps more homiletically viable. The typical pronouncement story has two parts: first, the pronouncement itself–a proverb, witticism, or rejoinder, in most cases a one-liner, and second, the context in which it occurs. Like a diamond set in a brooch, pronouncements are nestled in situations that both disclose how the pronouncement emerged and show off its brilliance.

By way of illustration, let us consider not a biblical pronouncement story but one of the more famous political anecdotes in American history. It is recounted that, after the Civil War, the renowned general, William Tecumseh Sherman, a man admired and very popular for his role in the Union victory, was pressured against his will by both political parties to present himself as a candidate for public office. Utterly disinterested in politics, the reluctant Sherman is said to have adamantly refused by saying, "If nominated, I will not run; if elected, I will not serve."[3]

This Sherman tale is clearly a cracking good pronouncement story; indeed, the only motive for remembering it or

---

[3]Alas, even relatively recent pronouncement stories have their textual variants, and the accounts differ as to Sherman's exact wording. Some have recorded his words as, "If nominated by either party, I should preemptorily decline, and even if unanimously elected, I should decline to serve"–not as compact or rhetorically effective as the above version, but perhaps more historically accurate.

retelling it is to get to the famous punch line: "If nominated, I will not run; if elected, I will not serve." When we think, however, about why this pronouncement possesses rhetorical power, three categories emerge:

1. *Poetics*–Sherman's quip in and of itself is well-crafted, symmetrical and rhythmic; plus it is at least mildly amusing, a 19th-century version of the country music hit "What part of 'no' don't you understand?"

2. *Transformation*–The statement significantly changes the context. The context was one of expectancy and desire (Sherman as our candidate!), but the statement reverses these ambitions by closing, locking, and double-bolting the door.

3. *Autonomy*–The story obviously depends upon an interplay between context and pronouncement, but, once uttered, the pronouncement possesses at least a limited autonomy. It can float free from its original context and attach itself to new and similar situations. Thus, potential candidates in our own time who seem to be shrinking from the political fray (a la Mario Cuomo) are pressed as to whether they are making "Sherman-like" statements.

Putting this together, then–and here is where the homiletical payoff begins–pronouncement stories contain rhetorically crafted statements that generate change in their contexts and have the capacity to generate similar change in new and analogous situations. Now let us see what the preacher is to do with this.

Preaching Pronouncement Stories

A sermon developed out of a pronouncement story text should be different from a sermon created on a miracle story, a psalm, or a parable. But how? Clearly, the task of the preacher is not to replicate the pronouncement structure. As we have seen, pronouncement stories are most often brief descriptions of a context followed by a one-line quip, but sermons are something else, something more. To put it perhaps too simply, the task of the preacher is not to imitate the pronouncement story form, but to regenerate its impact, to exegete it rhetorically and to create a sermon that does now something of what the original pronouncement did then.

The preacher, therefore, should consider pronouncement stories to be communicational events, transactions between a speaker and a hearer or between a narrator and a reader, and seek to construct similar communicational events in a new genre (the sermon) for a new audience (the hearers). As such, it is precisely the rhetorical categories named above–poetics, transformation, and autonomy–that can provide the necessary homiletical clues. To attend to poetics requires that the preacher discern the internal construction of the pronouncement; to attend to the matter of transformation opens up the ways in which the pronouncement impacts the context; and to attend to autonomy requires the preacher to make a hermeneutical shift from the Gospel setting to the contemporary.

In two fine essays in the experimental biblical journal *Semeia*,[4] Robert C. Tannehill explores the varieties of synoptic pronouncement stories, attempting to classify them according to their functions, that is in terms of the ways in which the "provoking occasion" (the context) is addressed by the "response" (the pronouncement). Thus, because Tannehill's categories seek to name the ways that synoptic pronouncements impact their literary environments and generate change in their contexts, they are quite instructive to the preacher.

In what follows, I will list the varieties of pronouncement stories as given by Tannehill and then, using examples of pronouncement stories drawn from the Gospel of Luke, explore how the preacher may approach each type:

1. Correction Stories–In a correction story, according to Tannehill, "the responder takes a position that contrasts with and corrects the position assumed through word or action by some other party."[5] In other words, the narrative part of the story sets up some kind of viewpoint—maybe it's conventional wisdom, maybe it's an attitude that seems innocent or commendable–but

---

[4] Robert C. Tannehill, "Introduction: The Pronouncement Story and Its Types" and "Varieties of Synoptic Pronouncement Stories," *Semeia* 20/1981, 1-13 and 101-119 respectively. This entire volume of Semeia is given over to biblical pronouncement stories and perhaps serves as the best introduction to this form for the preacher.

[5] Tannehill "Varieties of Synoptic Pronouncement Stories," 103-104.

whatever it is, the pronouncement comes along to knock it down. The narrative blows up a balloon, and the pronouncement quickly pops it!

An example of the correction type can be found in Luke 11:27-28. Jesus has just performed an exorcism and has been charged by some in the crowd with being in league with Beelzebub, the prince of demons. Jesus is responding to this charge and teaching about demonic possession when a woman suddenly steps forward out of the crowd and interrupts him, gushing, "Blessed is the womb that bore you and the breasts that nursed you!" In other words, "What a fine young man you are. I know your mother is proud!"

Now, at one level, there is nothing amiss here. This woman is simply saying what Jesus' own mother predicted would be said: "Surely, from now on all generations will call me blessed" (Luke 1:48). Indeed, it is only when Jesus responds with a statement of correction that we realize anything is wrong. "Blessed rather are those who hear the word of God and obey it!" he says, correcting her flattery.

The woman is correct that Jesus is a blessing, but she is wrong about why. In one way, she tells the truth–"Blessed is your mother"–but she is working out of corrupt categories. She thinks it is a blessing to be the blood kin, the natural mother, to such an impressive son, when in fact the true blessing comes to those who are kin by virtue of obedience to his word. She is operating according conventional standards of what makes for blessedness in this world; Jesus is redefining those categories, and she misses that point. What this pronouncement accomplishes is to make it clear, then, that Jesus faces two kinds of opponents: those who think he is a curse (an agent of Beelzebub) and, ironically, those who think in mistaken ways that he is a blessing.

A sermon on this pronouncement story would look to identify—and to bring under critique—all of the ways in which we rise up to praise Jesus and call ourselves blessed by him, but in fact are doing so out of cultural values. A well-told story has made the rounds about the Baptist preacher Carlisle Marney, who one day visited a fellow cleric and was treated to a tour of this minister's new church building. The minister pointed out the mahogany pews, the exquisite stained glass windows, the magnificent pulpit. For the coup de grace, Marney was led outside to look up at the soaring steeple, on top of which stood a cross. "That cross alone cost $25,000," cooed the minister. "Really? replied Marney. "Christians used to be able to get those for nothing." Blessed are those who inhabit alabaster sanctuaries in praise of Jesus? No. "Blessed rather are those who hear the word of God and obey it!"

2. Commendation Stories–A commendation story is a mirror image of the correction story "in that the responder responds to a position taken by another person.... [but in this case] the responder commends rather than corrects the other person."[6] The function, then, of the commendation story is to reinforce an attitude or a behavior that is worthy of the Gospel.

A rather longish example of a commendation story can be found in Luke 7:1-10, the account of the centurion whose slave was ill. The very length of this passage indicates that this is more than a simple pronouncement narrative, but it still bears the basic structure of pronouncements in that everything leads up to the clinching statement of Jesus: "I tell you, not even in Israel have I found such faith." Jesus validates and commends the centurion for his humility and willingness to submit.

This pronouncement story, then, provides the preacher with an opportunity to lift up examples of humility and obedience– especially perhaps those that occur outside the normal boundaries of faith, outside of "Israel"—and to commend them to the congregation.

For instance, once there was near the town where I live a small and fashionable grocery market. It is gone now, overwhelmed by the giant chains, but for years this store served the "carriage trade" in our area.

Every morning at about the same time a woman would enter this store and steal food. We'll call her "Ruth," and she was homeless. Ruth would wear a long overcoat, even on hot days, and she would move from aisle to aisle stuffing bread, cheese, packaged meat–whatever she could find to eat–under this coat. Everybody in the store knew what she was up to. The clerks knew, the stock boys knew; everybody knew that Ruth was stealing food.

It came to pass that this grocery store, in an attempt to

---

[6]Tannehill, "Introduction...," 7.

compete with the larger stores, moved to a new and bigger location, some blocks away from the original site. On the day of the move, the manager of the grocery called the pastor of one of the local churches and told her, "Look, we don't want to embarrass Ruth, but would you find a way to tell her about our new location. We don't want her to miss lunch." "I tell you, not even in Israel have I found such faith."

3. *Objection Stories*–The objection story is a close kin to the correction story, but with an important structural difference. In correction stories, someone expresses a view, which Jesus' statement corrects. In objection stories, however, someone is trying to correct Jesus, and the pronouncement is Jesus' response to this objection.

Objection stories, Tannehill notes, have three parts: "1) the cause of the objection, 2) the objection, which is sometimes expressed by a question..., and 3) the response to the objection."[7] A good example of this type can be found in the story of Mary and Martha in Luke 10:38-42. The story presents the cause of the objection (Martha sweats over the meal while Mary sits at Jesus' feet), the objection itself, voiced by Martha ("Lord, do you not care.... Tell her then to help me"), and the response of Jesus ("Martha, Martha, you are worried and distracted by many things; there is need of only one thing. Mary has chosen the better part, which will not be taken away from her.").

In this story, Martha has a criticism of Jesus. He ought to be more alert to her plight; he ought to care more about the exigencies of the meal, and he should order Mary to get up off the floor and to pick up her responsibilities at the oven. Jesus, however, corrects the correction by lifting up what Mary is doing—listening to the word—over all other human activities.

Thus, this type of story invites the preacher to think about times in our own day when people object to some aspect of the mission of Jesus, when they genuinely believe that Jesus should have been otherwise, taught otherwise, done otherwise and to explore what clarification and reaffirmation of that mission can be given. I remember attending a church event one evening when the program was a film depicting the life of Jesus in contemporary terms. The movie showed a man carrying a cross

---

[7]Ibid., 8.

through the streets of a busy modern city, only to encounter, much as Jesus himself, scorn, ridicule, and hostility. In one instance, had it not been for the intervention of the director and some security guards, the actor portraying Jesus would have been the victim of violence from those who found his presence offensive. When the film was over, the leader asked those of us present if we had any reactions to the movie. One woman stood up, trembling with rage, and sputtered, "That was a terrible way to tell the sweet story of Jesus." Perhaps the only response to her notion of the "sweet story of Jesus" would be another of Jesus' pronouncements: "Oh, how foolish you are....Was it not necessary that the Messiah should suffer..." (Luke 24:25-26).

4. Quest Stories–In a quest story, someone is seeking something. It may be healing for themselves, healing for others, a blessing, alms, salvation, or something else. What they get, however, is a pronouncement, which is usually not what the quester was seeking but, in fact, turns out to be more than they knew to ask for. Most pronouncement stories end with the pronouncement, since the making of the key statement is the goal of the story. Quest stories, however, add one more ingredient: it "discloses the need of the quester and comes to an end by announcing success or failure in meeting that need."[8]

The story of the rich ruler in Luke 18:18-25 is a fine example of a quest story. The man is on a quest: "What must I do to inherit eternal life?" But, at least on this occasion, the quest ends in sadness when Jesus calls on him to do what he is not willing to do: divest himself of his wealth. Then the pronouncement: "How hard it is for those who have wealth to enter the kingdom of God! Indeed it is easier for a camel to go through the eye of a needle than for someone who is rich to enter the kingdom of God."

This type of story opens up for the preacher the opportunity to think about what people are questing for in our time. In an age of religious seeking, people are looking for all kinds of spiritual and material blessings. Sometimes the Gospel says yes, sometimes the Gospel says no, and always the Gospel deepens the quest. In her book *Operating Instructions*, Anne Lamott tells about the "60 Minutes" show which included an interview by

---

[8]Tannehill, "Varieties...," 112.

46

Ed Bradley with a family of three who made a pilgrimage every year to the healing shrine at Lourdes. This family—a devout mother of about thirty, an older and painfully shy father, and their 10-year-old daughter with spina bifida—were on a quest for a blessing from God.

According to Lamott, in the interview Bradley was badgering the family for being so gullible:

> He said to the little girl, who was so weak she had to be firmly strapped into the wheelchair, "What do you pray for when you come?" and she said, looking at her father really lovingly, "I pray that my dad won't always have to feel so shy. It makes him feel so lonely." Which stopped old Ed in his tracks for about ten seconds. But then he looked back at the mother and said something to the effect that "year after year you spend thousands of dollars to come here, hoping for a miracle," and she just looked at her kid, shook her head, and said, "Oh, no, Ed, you don't get it—we got our miracle."[9]

This mother understood what Ed Bradley perhaps could not, that their quest had been satisfied with a miracle, not in the expected way, but in a deeper way.

5. *Inquiry Stories*—According to Tannehill, inquiry stories are rather simple in structure: questions followed by an answers. The answer does not challenge the assumptions of the questioner (as in the correction story variety) nor does it satisfy some grand quest (as in the quest type). The questioner simply seeks information, and the pronouncement provides it. Thus, "the dramatic conflict and tension between persons which characterize many of the other stories are largely lacking in the inquiries."[10]

The exchange between John the Baptist and various segments of the crowd in Luke 3:10-14 fits the inquiry pattern nicely. Citizens, tax collectors, and soldiers all step forward in

---

[9]Anne Lamott, *Operating Instructions: A Journal of My Son's First Year* (New York: Fawcett Columbine, 1993), 115-116.

[10]Tannehill, "Introduction...," 10.

response to John's preaching to ask, in their own ways, "What shall we do." John has answers for each of them, tailored to their respective circumstances.

If nothing else, the inquiry story beckons the preacher to take seriously the questions on the minds of those who show up for worship. David Letterman once described his television show by saying, "Think of it as the information highway without the information." In a time of theological and biblical amnesia, Letterman's quip could perhaps be uttered about the church, too. People have questions, and preachers should not disdain trying our best to address them. "Does God ever will the death of children?" "Is it possible to be in business today and live as a Christian?" "Is the Bible true?" "Do dogs and cats go to heaven?" "Why have I suffered so?" "Is it always possible to forgive?" "Is Christianity the only true faith?" These are not easy questions, and there are no simple answers. But they are the questions people bring, and they are worth a struggle in the pulpit.

6. Description Stories–Tannehill terms his final variety of pronouncement narratives "description stories" because these stories present some human situation in vivid detail, and the pronouncement makes some insightful descriptive observation about this situation. The pronouncement "may be humorous, highlighting something ridiculous or incongruous in the situation" or "[i]t may be poignant, highlighting the tragedy of human limitations or the fateful consequences of what has happened."[11]

We can see a description story at work in Luke 12:54-56. First Jesus presents the human situation: people are quite adept at interpreting weather signs ("You see a cloud rising in the west, you immediately say, 'It is going to rain'; and so it happens."). Then comes the observation: for all their ability to read the signs, they miss what God is doing right before their eyes ("You know how to interpret the appearance of earth and sky, but you do not know how to interpret the present time.").

Such a text invites the preacher to present some human situation that everyone recognizes, but then, seeing it through the lens of the Gospel, to disclose some aspect of it that remains

---

[11]Ibid., 11.

hidden from ordinary view. Barbara Brown Taylor told in one of her sermons about an experience she had as a priest in a downtown Atlanta church. She was in charge of adult education and would occasionally survey her congregation to see what sort of courses they preferred. The answer always came back "Bible study;" in every survey, the congregation overwhelmingly said they wanted more Bible study. So Taylor would phone Bible professors at a nearby seminary and arrange for them to teach courses on the Bible–but surprisingly the congregation would stay away in droves.

This was puzzling, since the people repeatedly said more Bible study was exactly what they wanted. Then it dawned on Taylor that what they really wanted was not Bible study, but God. They really wanted an experience of the holy, and saying "more Bible study" was the only way they knew to express this hunger. So, Taylor began to plan a new kind of Bible study, explorations of the Bible that didn't stop with the textual details but spoke to the desire to know God and to draw closer to God's Spirit. To this, the people responded enthusiastically.

Notice that here a minister took a human situation and, after seeing only the surface, finally looked to the depths. This is precisely the dynamic of the description form of the pronouncement story.

Conclusion

The Gospels are filled with pronouncement stories. The early church clearly saw Jesus as one whose statements were provocative and of abiding worth, and they preserved many of them in the pronouncement form. Though many of us who preach are tempted to run the other direction when we stumble across one of these stories, being attending to the rhetorical functions of the pronouncement narratives and, with the help of scholars like Tannehill, being alert to the many nuances and wide variety present in the pronouncement form, the preacher can move a long way toward recovering the power of this literary form for today's pulpit.

Chapter Three:
Tale of Two Searchers

Luke's Use of Contrasting Pairs

> It was the best of times, it was the worst of times, it was
> the age of wisdom, it was the age of foolishness, it was
> the epoch of belief, it was the epoch of incredulity, it
> was the season of Light, it was the season of Darkness,
> it was the spring of hope, it was the winter of despair, we
> had everything before us, we had nothing before us, we
> were all going direct to Heaven, we were all going direct
> the other way....

These striking contrasts from the first sentence of Charles
Dickens' Tale of Two Cities may be the best-known
example of contrasts in English literature. In Scripture, Luke
rivals Dickens in contrasts. This is especially true when
looking at the theme of possessions. The living contrast between
the rich and the poor is given powerful literary
expression from the very beginning of the Gospel. Mary sings
the contrast in the Magnificat: "He has brought down the
powerful from their thrones, and lifted up the lowly; he has
filled the hungry with good things, and sent the rich away
empty" (Luke 1:52-53). Jesus uses stinging contrasts to
emphasize the reversal of fortunes awaiting the rich and poor,
"Blessed are you who are poor, for yours is the kingdom of
God... But woe to you who are rich, for you have received your
consolation" (6:20, 24) and "Blessed are you who are hungry
now, for you will be filled...Woe to you who are full now, for
you will be hungry" (6:21, 25).

Characters are also contrasted in many of the narrative
units unique to Luke, as in Simon and the sinful woman
(Luke 7:36-50) or Barnabas over against Ananias and Sapphira

(Acts 4:32-5:11). Within the parables of Jesus found only in Luke, one can easily find contrasts such as those between the rich man and Lazarus (Luke 16:19-31) or the Pharisee and the tax collector (Luke 18:9-14). Here, Luke's contrasts are about as straightforward as Dickens'famous opening sentence and reside within the same narrative units.

Other contrasts, however, are subtler. Take, for example, the centurion in Luke 7:1-10 and the widow of Nain in Luke 7:11-16. These characters are found in sequential texts rather than in the same narrative unit but it seems clear that Luke intends that his readers view them as a contrasting pair. One is a man of wealth and the other a desperately poor widow. In fact, Luke has already prepared us for this contrast in 4:25-28 where Jesus speaks of the impoverished widow of Zarephath and Naaman, the wealthy Syrian soldier. The contrast will return in Acts 9:36–10:48 where we first find Tabitha (Dorcas) and the widows and then the Centurion, Cornelius. In all of these cases, the contrasts of gender and wealth are extreme but they are not contrasted in their response to the message of the Kingdom. Luke portrays each of them in a favorable light.

Luke often contrasts a character in one narrative unit with one in a later unit, not in wealth or gender, but precisely in their response to the message of the Kingdom.[1] Such is the case in his descriptions of the Rich Ruler and Zacchaeus. Though both are rich men, and both seek Jesus, they are polar opposites in terms of their place in society and in how they respond to Jesus. The contrast is so sharp that it is appropriate to employ the language of Dickens and see the narratives as "The Tale of Two Searchers."

The Rich Ruler

The story of the rich ruler is not unique to Luke, but a

---

[1]In a less striking sense, Zechariah, whose unbelief is punished, is contrasted to Mary, who believes the angelic message in Luke 1. These contrasts continue in the book of Acts and are one of the important ways Luke's theology of possessions continues in his second volume. It has already been noted that Barnabas is contrasted with Ananias and Sapphira. Other much less recognized contrasts include Simon the Magician and the Ethiopian treasurer in Acts 8, Lydia and the Philippian slave owners in Acts 16, and the Ephesian Christians who burn their magic books over against the silver smiths in Acts 19.

comparison of Luke and Mark is revealing.[2] In both Mark and Luke, this text follows the story of the children coming to Jesus. However, Luke connects the saying about children directly to the question asked by the rich ruler, making the contrast between the children and the rich ruler sharp and immediate. Luke alone calls the man a ruler, further sharpening the contrast with children. The reader of Luke should avoid reading Matthew's "young man" into the story.

While in Mark, Jesus' words are, "sell what you have" (Mark 10:21) in Luke Jesus says, "Sell all that you have" (Luke 18:22). Mark describes the man as one who "had great possessions" (Mark 10:22) while Luke simply says, "he was very rich" (Luke 18:23). These changes serve to focus attention on the theme of possessions even more sharply than in Mark.

In Mark's account, the man left with great sorrow (Mark 10:22). In Luke, however, there is no mention of his leaving, giving the impression that Jesus addressed the saying on how hard it is for those who have riches to enter the kingdom of God directly to the ruler. Luke leaves out Mark's description of the disciples' amazement and moves directly to the proverb of the camel through the needle's eye (Luke 18:25).[3] This, too, would presumably be directed to the ruler. Only then is a larger audience mentioned ("those who heard it"–Luke 18:26).

Luke's narrative invites the reader to see the rich ruler as a personification of the Rich Fool (12:13-21), and gives flesh and blood to the warning: "What does it profit a man if he gains the whole world and loses or forfeits himself?" (9:25). The rich man's unwillingness to surrender his wealth vividly illustrates Luke's theology of possessions.

The text presents the difficult question of whether all disciples are expected literally to sell everything. Luke does

---

[2]This paper assumes that the "two-document hypothesis" is, in broad outline, correct. For a recent discussion of the sources behind Luke, see Joseph B. Tyson, "Source Criticism of the Gospel of Luke," *Perspectives On Luke-Acts*, ed. Charles H. Talbert (Edinburgh: T. & T. Clark, 1978), 24-39.

[3]Virtually all scholars today see "camel through the eye of a needle" as referring to both a literal camel and a literal sewing needle, not as a reference to a gate in the wall surrounding Jerusalem. The point to the hyperbole is not in the difficulty but in the impossibility of the rich being saved apart from a Divine act of grace, as the text makes clear.

emphasize that the rich man was to sell all his possessions (18:22), but is that the paradigm for discipleship? The problem with a straightforward answer is that some of Jesus' followers were, and remained, rich. One can think of Joseph of Arimathaea, Mary and Martha, and all those who continued to support the ministry of Jesus out of their means.[4] One also thinks of Levi, who is said to have left everything and followed Jesus (5:28). Yet, after leaving everything, he held a "great feast" in his house. Further examples appear in Acts. Wealthy women like Mary, the mother of Mark (Acts 12:12) and Lydia (Acts 16:15) opened their houses for the church. Others gave out of the means they still possessed to serve the church. Luke T. Johnson pursues the implication of that evidence:

> Side by side with the call to total renunciation of possessions, therefore, we find the ideal of almsgiving and hospitality. A simple but important point must be made about this. If the two practices are not mutually exclusive, they are at least impossible to practice at one and the same time.[5]

If all disciples were called to do what this man was called to do, all would be among "the needy and wandering." While Luke does not say that the demand upon the rich ruler is unique, neither does he say that it is normative. Even among the twelve the call was not identical to the one given this rich ruler. The fishermen (Luke 5:11) left all and followed Jesus, but they apparently did not sell all and give the proceeds to the poor before following Jesus. In fact, Mark's gospel makes it clear that Jesus ministered out of Peter's house (Mark 1:29-34). In Luke, while Peter and the other disciples leave their homes, there is no suggestion that Peter left his wife and mother-in-law homeless.

The parallels between the story of the rich ruler and the warnings in Luke 16:10-17 are significant. Like the Pharisees of 16:14, this rich man was a "lover of money." Like them, he

---

[4]Luke mentions women who supported Jesus: "Mary, called Magdalene, from whom seven demons had gone out, 3 and Joanna, the wife of Herod's steward Chuza, and Susanna, and many others, who provided for them out of their resources." (Luke 8:2-3).

[5]L. T. Johnson, *Sharing Possessions: Mandate and Symbol of Faith* (Philadelphia: Fortress Press, 1981), 20.

could not serve two masters (16:13). He also was devoted to the law (16:16-17). The list of commandments the rich man claimed to have followed is from the second table of the law, those dealing with interpersonal ethics. However, the man's fundamental problem was not from the second table, but the first table. In fact, it was the first commandment he was failing to keep, the one prohibiting idolatry. Wealth became this man's idol. He tried to serve God and mammon. Like the Pharisees of Luke 16, he may have thought that his possessions were a mark of God's favor. Like them, he finally, although sorrowfully, rejected the call of Jesus to the kingdom.

The man was told that he must completely give up his idolatrous relationship with wealth if he was to inherit eternal life. There is no wonder, then, that it is so hard for the rich to enter the kingdom (18:24). It is indeed so hard that it is impossible with men (18:25, 26) and must come from God (18:27). It must be the gracious gift of the one who calls, and yet it must be met by the surrendering of all.

Although the specifics of the call differ from those in other cases, the rich ruler was not called to discipleship on a different basis than others. The basis is the same as that expressed in Luke 14:33, "So therefore, whoever of you does not renounce all that he has cannot be my disciple." As I have elsewhere argued, this saying does not require the universal and physical dispossession by all disciples but it does require renouncing the ownership of all possessions by all disciples.[6] The story of the rich ruler demonstrates just how serious that renunciation is. Not all were called to sell everything, but each disciple needed to know that none "of the things which he possessed was his own" (Acts 4:32).

The Blind Beggar

The text of the blind man of Jericho stands in its own right as a story of one who is healed and becomes a follower of Jesus. However, it also serves as a narrative bridge between the story of the rich ruler and the story of Zacchaeus. Located where it is, the story both bridges and stands in contrast to those texts. The ruler was exceedingly rich but unwilling to renounce his wealth.

---

[6]See "Renounce Your Possessions," *Leaven*, 6 (Summer, 1998).

Zacchaeus was also rich but he was willing to part with his wealth. The blind man was a poor beggar who has nothing from which to part, but found healing and more.

The blind man cried only for mercy. His faith in the "Son of David," unlike the ultimate unbelief of the rich ruler, made him well. Unlike that ruler, this poor, blind beggar "received his sight and followed him, glorifying God" (18:43). That is the language of the disciple, and it illustrates perfectly what was promised in the program statement of Luke 4:16-30: "…good news to the poor … sight to the blind."

While the story of the rich ruler illustrates how hard it is for the rich to enter the kingdom of God, this story illustrates how the poor are blessed because the kingdom of God is theirs (6:20). It also prepares the reader for the remarkable story of Zacchaeus, which illustrates that all things are possible for God.

Zacchaeus

Walter Pilgrim goes so far as to say, "We regard the story of Zacchaeus as the most important Lukan text on the subject of the right use of possessions."[7] However, as in the story of the rich ruler, questions arise regarding possessions and the call of the kingdom. Was a different demand given to Zacchaeus than to the ruler? Did Zacchaeus give up only a portion of his wealth or all that he had? Is he indeed the "paradigm par excellence for Luke of how the rich can enter the kingdom of God," as Pilgrim suggests?[8] If so, how is that paradigm to be copied?

Two different strains of Luke's narrative converge in this text. Luke's thoroughly sympathetic portrayal of tax collectors contrasts sharply with his portrayal of the rich, who are consistently pictured as those who have received their reward and stand in danger of a reversal of fortune by the judgment of God (1:51, 6:24, 12:16-21, 16:19-31). Up to this point in Luke the only person specifically called "rich" who is described in a way not overtly negative is the master of the dishonest steward (16:1).

In the story of Zacchaeus, therefore, Luke has brought two conflicting portrayals into one character. That he is a tax

---

[7]W. E. Pilgrim, *Good News to the Poor: Wealth and Poverty in Luke-Acts* (Minneapolis: Augsburg, 1981), 129.

[8]Ibid., 134.

collector suggests that he, as other tax collectors have, will respond positively to Jesus. That he is rich suggests that he will not. As the narrative progresses, it is clear that the expectation of those within the story is the reverse of the expectation the reader will have brought to the story. The reader might expect Luke to denounce him for his wealth while the crowd condemns him for being a tax collector. Neither expectation is met.

Zacchaeus responds to the crowd's accusation: "Behold, Lord, the half of my goods I give to the poor; and if I have defrauded anyone of anything, I restore it fourfold" (19:8). Zacchaeus' willingness to give half of his possessions to the poor clearly goes far beyond common generosity. To repay four-fold follows the restitution demanded of one who has stolen sheep (Exodus 22:1). Yet, is it the same as giving all? Whether one makes that assumption largely depends upon how dishonest one believes Zacchaeus to have been. What is clear is that, unlike the story of the rich ruler, Jesus did not demand that Zacchaeus do anything with his possessions. Zacchaeus volunteers this response to Jesus' gracious offer of table fellowship. While we can speculate that Zacchaeus had been dishonest enough for this response to leave him impoverished the text does not say so. As Luke T. Johnson observes, Zacchaeus "clearly has not impoverished himself (half a bundle can still be a bundle)."[9]

In Luke 18:28, in response to his statements on the impossibility of a rich man being saved, Jesus is asked, "Then who can be saved?" The story of Zacchaeus answers that question. Even a rich chief tax collector can be saved. Whether he actually disposes of all his possessions is secondary; that Jesus promises salvation to his house proves that he has renounced his possessions in the sense in which Jesus required (Luke 14:33).

All are to renounce all of their possessions. Having come to the kingdom of God, both they and all they have are subject to the Lord. What differs from case to case is how those possessions will be used. In this respect, the particulars of Zacchaeus's response may differ from that required of the rich

---

[9] L. T. Johnson, *The Gospel of Luke, Sacra Pagina Series*, vol. 3 (Collegeville, MN: The Liturgical Press), 1991, 286. *In Sharing Possessions: Mandate and Symbol of Faith* (Philadelphia: Fortress Press, 1981), 20, Johnson says, "This is an extraordinarily generous response, it is true, but not absolute renunciation. ... We are not told that he sold his house, left all his possessions, and followed Jesus, or even stopped being a tax collector."

ruler. Nevertheless, Zacchaeus disposed of much–perhaps all–of his wealth for the benefit of the poor and for restitution to any whom he had defrauded. He was accepted by Jesus, and in response met the demands of the kingdom. In light of this, Jesus declared, "Today salvation has come to this house" (Luke 19:9).

Exploring the Contrast

To understand Luke's purposes in these contrasting narratives it is vital to see their social and religious context. While wealth was one aspect of social status, it was not the only or even the most important aspect. How a person acquired wealth was crucial.[10] Tax collectors, though often wealthy, were businessmen of a low status. As is clear in many gospel narratives, they were placed alongside sinners. The rich ruler, on the other hand, not only had wealth but also had high social status. His religious devotion to the law gave to him honor and regard. His wealth was seen as God's blessing. Based on contemporary social values, the two would be seen in radically different ways. To return to the language of Dickens, the rich ruler and Zacchaeus could be seen as "The best of all seekers and the worst of all seekers."

It would be hard to imagine a greater boost for the ministry of Jesus in the world in which he moved than to have a wealthy ruler as both disciple and patron. It would also be a boost to the status of Jesus' ministry for him to reject the approach of Zacchaeus. Jesus' welcome of tax collectors and "sinners" was a scandal Jesus found necessary to defend (Luke 15). In Luke, Simon the Pharisee is representative of the reaction Jesus gets when he accepts sinners. Simon, who hosts Jesus, is scandalized not only by the presence of a woman he knows as a "sinner" but also by Jesus' acceptance of her lavish attention to him. If he were really a prophet he would not only know about her but also reject her.

Luke's narrative shows us just how thoroughly Jesus turned the social/religious values of his world "upside down."[11] Jesus' refusal to invite the rich ruler to be his disciple on any condition

---

[10]See, John E. Stambaugh and David L. Balch, *The New Testament in its Social Environment* (Philadelphia: Westminster Press, 1986), 77-78.

[11]This of course was the accusation made against Paul and his companions in Thessalonica in Acts 17:6, "These people who have been turning the world upside down have come here also."

less than a complete renunciation of his possessions is a rejection of the theology of wealth held by many. The rich man's wealth was not evidence of God's blessing; it was instead evidence of the man's idolatry. Zacchaeus, on the other hand, was deeply despised on religious and political grounds. Whereas the rich ruler would have been considered a true heir of his wealthy patriarch, Abraham, Zacchaeus would have been viewed as one who forfeited his claim to Abraham altogether. Certainly, it would have been assumed, no true child of Abraham would sell out his own people to collect taxes for Rome! The diminutive Zacchaeus must climb a tree, not simply because he is a "wee, little man" but because the crowd will not let this despised traitor, in spite of his wealth, to a place where he could see. The people's hostility toward Zacchaeus quickly attaches itself to Jesus. Instead of condemning Zacchaeus, Jesus has arranged to have table-fellowship with this sinner in the sinner's own home.[12]

From Text to Pulpit

There may be a no more discomforting theme in Luke/Acts for contemporary Americans than that of possessions. All of us, without exception, have been immersed in a culture that measures worth by fame and wealth. The popular bumper sticker "The One Who Dies With The Most Toys Wins," is a crass, but accurate reflection of our age. From the right to "Life, Liberty, and the Pursuit of Happiness" we seem to have added the right to two cars, three televisions, a new computer, and a swimming pool outside of our two-story home. Items once considered "luxuries" are now seen as necessities. It seems the rule now that even people calling churches for financial assistance leave their cell-phone and pager numbers so that we can contact them. America as the land of opportunity has come to mean the opportunity to make money, not the opportunity to enjoy religious liberty.

A consumer culture dominates our lives. It is certainly felt in churches. Denominational and sectarian loyalties are rapidly disappearing and giving way to the search for churches that meet

---

[12] Note the complaint in Luke 15:1-2, "Now all the tax collectors and sinners were coming near to listen to him. And the Pharisees and the scribes were grumbling and saying, 'This fellow welcomes sinners and eats with them.'" For a discussion of the implications of table-fellowship, see Halvor Moxness, *The Economy of the Kingdom: Social Conflict and Economic Relations in Luke's Gospel* (Philadelphia: Fortress Press, 1988), see especially 99-105.

people's needs. Often these are upscale suburban churches that offer engaging worship services. Worship in these churches tends to promise comfort, affirmation, and little in the way of serious theology. The view of God as Giver, both of salvation and material prosperity, appears to dominate. How can the preacher listen to these texts, let alone proclaim them in this culture? How do we take seriously the call to renounce possessions when the entire culture preaches accumulate possessions? How do we affirm in worship, what is so roundly rejected everywhere else? We can talk about being generous but the words of Jesus in Luke go beyond generosity. We can speak of giving, and do so constantly, but can we talk of surrendering ownership of all that we have?

These are not trivial questions for the preacher and they come to us in intensely personal ways. We are not outsiders commenting on the materialism of our age. We, too, are enmeshed in this culture. Our families depend upon the salaries we make preaching to churches who often demand "consumer satisfaction." While we may speak out against the sexual immorality and violence within the popular culture and win the approval of our congregations, it is not at all clear that we can seriously speak against the materialism of our culture and expect the same response. We look out at our own sisters and brothers and see those who are so caught up in consuming careers that their presence in a pew and a sizable check in the contribution plate is all we can expect from them. We look at working couples, struggling to make their second or third mortgages because they are determined to give their children "enough." We look at divorced, single mothers who refuse to go on welfare and work long hours to fill the holes left by the deadbeat dads who checked out of their lives. We look at a people who, largely, have never considered that their love of their Sports Utility Vehicles might in any way be in competition with their love of the Lord.

For us, the story of the rich ruler is manageable only if we can put enough distance between the text and ourselves. Only when we can say, "he is not me" can we deal with this story. One way this has been done is to lay the story beside the story of Abraham's willingness to sacrifice Isaac. Here, the preacher says something like, "Just as God stayed Abraham's hand once it was clear that he really was willing to sacrifice Isaac, so Jesus would have 'stayed the hand' of the ruler once He saw that the ruler really would have sold all that he had." In this telling (which I have heard), we are to imagine Jesus saying, "Now that I know you would have given all away, I allow you to keep your wealth as long as you don't love it." The preacher continues, "the tragedy is, however, that he loved his wealth too much and Jesus could never give that gracious word!" The application is then made that we may accumulate wealth but we must never love it. The story, having been properly defanged, is safe to preach and the congregation can then return to their secular houses of worship and give themselves to Mammon.

In the same way, the story of Zacchaeus is made a story of determination to achieve a goal. The point is that if we have a goal we should let nothing get in the way of our dreams. "Zacchaeus was short of stature but large of heart and overcame his disadvantage by determination. The story becomes "Christian" only in that he wanted to see Jesus, and "Jesus, like God," we may say, "will reward such human determination."[13] Such a transformation into a tale compatible with modern humanism may be hermeneutic blasphemy but it also keeps Luke's real point at arm's length. Dare we talk of Zacchaeus' willingness, even joy, at the prospect of divesting himself of the damning weight of his wealth?

These two stories challenge our fundamental cultural values in the same way that Jesus challenged the cultural values of his day. While I will suggest some practical steps we may take in preaching these texts and other Lukan texts about possessions, I cannot escape one primary conclusion. It takes courage to preach. It is the courage Jesus demonstrated in his own cultural setting in the face of a dominant religious culture whom Luke describes as "lovers of money" (Luke 16:14). It takes more courage to face ourselves in this light and acknowledge that we are very much a part of the dominant culture of our day.

In part, then, preaching from these texts must be confessional. The finest example of this I have ever heard was Dr. Jack Reese's powerful sermon at Pepperdine's 1998 Bible

---

[13] For this interpretation, see William Barclay, *The Gospel of Luke*. The Daily Bible Study Series, Philadelphia: Westminster Press, 1955, 244. To be fair, Barclay goes beyond this reading, but many sermons have not.

Lectureship.[14] The sermon's power was, in large measure, due to its confessional nature. He confessed that he was, and by implication, all of us are, "rich" by any reasonable measure. Neither he, nor we who heard him, could hide from these penetrating texts. He did not push us but escorted us into the message of Luke. If we were condemned by his words, we knew that he already acknowledged his own guilt. This cannot be a homiletic manipulation. If repentance is to follow confession, we who preach must be first in line.

At some level, sermons on these texts need to bridge the cultural gap between the world of the Gospel and our own world. While there are strong dissimilarities between our worlds, the goal is to make appropriate connections so that we can find ourselves in these stories. To whom can we compare the rich ruler? Here, again, we must be careful not to suggest a comparison that excludes the congregation. The powerful young billionaire on the cover of *Forbes* will likely be a poor choice. He may be admired in our world as the rich ruler was in Jesus' world but too many connections will be missing. Immediately, such a comparison distances the ruler from the hearer: "Since I'm hardly likely to grace the cover of *Forbes*, he's talking about someone else." Much of the Gospel story's power is found in the man's devotion to keeping the law. He is not only wealthy; he is devout and sincere. If we are to see this person as the first readers of Luke saw him, we need to see him as thoroughly admirable. He is someone we want to be like. He is the searcher who comes to our church looking for the one answer to complete his quest for eternal life. He is someone so completely admirable that everyone would say in unison, "Look, here is water! What is to prevent him from being baptized?" Only then can we sense the shock of Jesus' call and the man's rejection of discipleship on those terms.

A proper comparison for Zacchaeus presents exactly the opposite problem. From childhood, many in our congregations have sung about this "wee little man" who climbed the sycamore tree. Our mental image has been that of a delightful little "Munchkin" with the face of Fantasy Island's Tatoo, sitting

[14] See Jack Reese, "Tearing Down and Building Bigger," *Leaven*, 6 (Summer, 1998): 108-112.

in the tree crying "De Lord, De Lord!" With such an image, it is hard to understand that Zacchaeus was a pariah in his own city. Instead, we need to see him as one who would cause many to want to drain the baptistery before he could reach it. He is the used car salesman, personal injury lawyer, county tax assessor, abortion doctor, and communist party member all rolled into one. If the wealth of the rich ruler brought admiration from the community, the wealth of Zacchaeus only made their blood boil. His gold rings and flowing robes were seen as the rewards of his traitorous exploitation of his own people.

Both the rich ruler and Zacchaeus, with all of their possibilities for preaching, present the preacher with serious difficulties in making connections with the contemporary church. My own inclination is to tell Luke's story rather than trying to create a contemporary story that conveys the same message. Yet, modern analogies are essential if these stories are to make meaningful, emotional connections. In the end, the story of the rich ruler should make the modern middle-class suburbanite seriously consider that he or she might be the rich ruler, not by the amount of their wealth but by their love of it. The story of Zacchaeus should also connect, not only with wealthy outcasts, but also with anyone who longs for acceptance by God and community with the "children of Abraham." All of us who live with the culture of possessions should see in the story that it is possible still to let go of our possessions with real joy.

One possibility lies close at hand for us. Haven't all of us who have served in ministry for some years known of someone we were sure would be both a positive addition to the church and, by the way, a feather in our cap. Haven't we found ourselves salivating over a prospective convert because he or she brought prestige with them as a bonus? Haven't we, to our embarrassment and perhaps shame, dismissed someone as a "poor" prospect only to find that the Lord knew better than we did? The problem with sharing those stories is that we are not the heroes. These stories place us amongst those who couldn't believe that Jesus would push the demands of discipleship so far to the ruler and among those who were upset that Jesus so graciously and enthusiastically embraced the tax man. So, be it! Our failure stories place us just where the texts can interpret us and allow the congregation to be interpreted as well, so that we can be shaped by the values of the Kingdom.

None of this is easy. The challenges cannot be met by a homiletical bag of tricks. Rather let there be an awkward confession than a glib sermon. Better yet, a prayerfully and thoughtfully crafted sermon that places us all before these powerful stories and gives us all, preacher and church, the freedom to repent.

Chapter Four
"Pray Always":
Prayer in Luke/Acts

G REG S TERLING

The third evangelist has been appropriately called "the evangelist of prayer."[1] While the other evangelists mention prayer, none of them develop the concept as fully as Luke does.[2] This is evident in multiple ways. Luke makes more references to prayer than the other evangelists. He uses a larger vocabulary and typically uses the common words more frequently than his counterparts (see the Appendix).The extensive vocabulary and frequency of use reflect a deliberate expansion of the motif in his sources, Q and Mark: the third evangelist has only taken over thirteen expressions from Q[3] and seven from Mark.[4] The remain-

---

[1]The earliest reference that I am aware of is that of P. Samain, *Revue du diocèse de Tournai* 3 (1947) 422-26. L. Monloubou, *La prière selon Saint Luc: Recherche d'une struc - ture* (Lectio Divina 89; Paris: Cerf, 1976) 19 n. 2, provides a brief sketch of its origins. The phrase has become a commonplace in works in the second half of the twentieth century.

[2]I use the traditional names for the evangelists in this article by convention only.

[3]αἰτέω from Q in Matt 7:7, 8, 9, 10, 11//Luke 11:9, 10, 11, 12, 13; δέομαι from Q in Matt 9:38//Luke 10:2; ἐξομολογέομαι from Q in Matt 11:25//Luke 10:21; ζητέω from Q in Matt 7:7,8//Luke 11:9,10; κρούω from Q in Matt 7:7, 8//Luke 11:9, 10; προσεύχομαι from Q in Matt 5:44//Luke 6:28; Matt 6:9//Luke 11:2. The occurrence of εὐλογέω in Luke 6:28 may come from Q (Matt 5:44//Luke 6:28), but it does not appear in the Matthean version.

[4]εὐλογέω from Mark 6:41 in Luke 9:16; εὐχαριστέω from Mark 14:23 in Luke 22:17; προσεύχομαι from Mark 12:40//Luke 20:47; Mark 14:32//Luke 22:40; Mark 14:35//Luke 22:41; Mark 14:38//Luke 22:46; and προσευχή from Mark 11:17 in Luke 19:46. Luke omit-ted αἰτέω at Mark 11:24 since it is part of the cursing of the fig tree episode that he found problematic (see also below). He omitted two of the Markan uses of εὐλογέω for prayer: Mark 8:7 which is part of the "big omission" (Mark 6:45-8:26 at Luke 9:17) and Mark 14:22 where Luke has replaced it with εὐχαριστέω (Luke 22:19). Luke omitted εὐχαριστέω at Mark 8:6 since it is part of the big omission. He omitted six of Mark's ten uses of προσεύ-'χομαι: Mark 1:35 dropped at Luke 4:42 since it does not fit the pattern that Luke carefully develops for prayer in the life of Jesus (see below); Mark 6:46 since it is part of the big

ing twenty-seven references in Luke are either from special sources or from the pen of the evangelist. This means that 57% of the references in Luke are unique to the third evangelist. The same pattern is even more pronounced when we consider the prayers that each evangelist records. Mark has two prayers;[5] Matthew has four (two from Q and two from Mark);[6] Luke has ten and only four of these come from Q and Mark.[7]

Luke does more than expand earlier treatments, he expands the material systematically. On two different occasions in the gospel the evangelist gathered material to create small manuals on prayer.[8] The only similar treatment is Matthew's treatment of prayer in the Sermon on the Mount.[9] Yet even here, there is a difference. The third evangelist makes his didactic purpose explicit through editorial introductions: in the former a disciple asked Jesus, "Lord teach us to pray just as John taught his disciples"; in the latter, the evangelist introduced the parable with "he told them a parable so that they would always pray and not give up."[10] Matthew is not this deliberate. The self-conscious nature of these collections is also evident in the narrative contexts in which Luke expands his sources. He does not arbitrarily expand the references to prayer by adding such references where they might be appropriate to a given story, but situates the references strategically in order to develop a thematic concern of the entire work. For example, the gospel

---

omission; Mark 11:24, 25 since they are part of the cursing of the fig tree pericope; Mark 13:18//Luke 21:23 since it does not fit with a major theme in Luke's development of prayer; Mark 14:39 since Luke completely rewrites the Gethsemane scene to remove the emotional struggle of Jesus (see below). Luke omitted προσευχή once: Mark 9:29 is omitted at Luke 9:43. This may be Luke's attempt to separate prayer from exorcism.

[5]Mark 14;36, Jesus in Gethsemane; 15:34, Jesus on the cross.

[6]Matthew takes over prayers from Q in Matt 11:25//Luke 10:21 and Matt 6:9-13//Luke 11:2-4. He takes over prayers from Mark 14:36//Matt 26:39 and Mark 15:34//Matt 27:46.

[7]Luke 2:29-32, Simeon; 10:21(-22)//Matt 11:25 (=Q), Jesus; 11:2-4//Matt 6:9-13 (=Q), Paternoster; 18:11-12, Pharisee; 18:13, tax-collector; 22:42//Mark 14:36 (=Mark), Jesus; 23:46, Jesus (this is a replacement for Mark 15:34); Acts 1:24-25, disciples; 4:24-30, disciples; 7:59-60, Stephen.

[8]Luke 11:1-13; 18:1-14.

[9]Matt 6:7-15.

[10]Luke 11:1; 18:1.

opens and closes and Acts opens with references to prayer.[11] Just as the evangelist has carefully located the events in these three texts in Jerusalem, so he has included prayer in all three.

But why? What purpose(s) do these references to prayer serve? Previous researchers have made numerous suggestions. Some have thought that prayer is a remedy for apostasy during the delayed or absent parousia.[12] Others have acknowledged this aspect but stressed the connection between prayer and the revelation of salvation history.[13] Still others have contended that prayer makes a Christological claim that Jesus is God's agent.[14] Yet others have claimed that prayer is the life of piety in the eschatological age.[15] The range of these views suggests that prayer may have more than a single function.[16]

The difficulty lies in part with the fact that the author has written a narrative. Themes are embedded in diverse stories and not treated systematically by the author even in texts that collect material with common themes. Each story presents what is necessary for the individual story, but does not present a full account of any given theme. What we must look for are patterns. I suggest that prayer intersects with three major themes of Luke/Acts: it portrays the Jewish character of early Christian piety in keeping with the argument that Christianity is the continuation of Israel, it provides an antidote to apostasy in

---

[11]Luke 1:10; 24:53; Acts 1:14.

[12]W. Ott, *Gebet und Heil: Die Bedeutung der Gebetsparänese in der lukanischen Theologie* (Studien zum Alten und Neuen Testament 12; München: Kösel, 1965) and J. A. Fitzmyer, *The Gospel According to Luke* (AB 28 & 28A; Garden City, New York: Doubleday, 1981-85) 1:244-47, esp. 247.

[13]O. G. Harris, "Prayer in Luke-Acts," 2-3, where he states his thesis; H. M. Conn, "Luke's Theology of Prayer," *Christianity Today* 17 (1972) 290-92; P. T. O'Brien, "Prayer in Luke-Acts," *Tyndale Bulletin* 24 (1973) 111-27, esp. 127; S. Smalley, "Spirit, Kingdom and Prayer in Luke-Acts," *NovT* 15 (1973) 59-71; A. Trites, "The Prayer Motif in Luke-Acts," in *Perspectives on Luke-Acts* (ed. C. H. Talbert; Danville, VA: Association of Baptist Professors of Religion, 1978) 168-86; S. F. Plymale, "Luke's Theology of Prayer," *SBLSP* (1990) 529-51; and *idem, The Prayer Texts of Luke-Acts* (New York: Peter Lang, 1992).

[14]L. Feldkämper, *Der betende Jesus als Heilsmittler nach Lukas* (Veröffentlichungen des Missionspriesterseminars St. Augustin bei Bonn 29; St. Augustin: Steyler, 1978).

[15]Fuhrman, "A Redactional Study of Prayer in the Gospel of Luke" 283.

[16]Besides the works mentioned in the notes above see also L. O. Harris, "Prayer in the Gospel of Luke," *Southwestern Journal of Theology* 10 (1967) 59-69 and J. Navone, *Themes of St. Luke* (Rome: Gregorian University Press, 1970), who survey the data without taking explicit positions in the debate.

the long view of salvation history, and it enables humans to understand or accept the plan of God that governs salvation history. These three themes serve as genetic strands around which the majority of the references to prayer cluster.

Prayer as Piety

The first of these concerns lay in the evangelist's attempt to associate Christianity with Israel. Writing at the end of the first century CE, the evangelist had to address the relationship between Christianity and Judaism. The large scale inclusion of Gentiles into Christianity raised the question whether Christianity was a movement within Judaism or a new and distinct movement. All of the gospels written towards the end of the century addressed the issue. Matthew recognized the widening chasm between the two; John treated the break as a *fait accompli*. The third evangelist argued that Christianity was a continuation of Israel, not a new movement. This is evident in numerous ways, e.g., the imitation of the style of the LXX, the insistence that the narrative is a fulfillment narrative of prophecy, and the centrality of Jerusalem as the beginning point of the movement. The argument was important for numerous reasons. Historically Christianity developed out of Judaism and yet it had evolved into something different. The argument for continuity allowed the author to claim identification with past Israel and separation from contemporary Judaism simultaneously. Further, the author could not admit that Christianity was new without losing the protective cover that Judaism afforded both socially and politically. It was therefore critical that the evangelist present Christianity as a recognizable heir of Israel.

As we have already suggested, the argument unfolds in many different ways: prayer is one of them. The argument is not simply that Christians prayed: almost everyone in the ancient world prayed and prayed in similar ways. The argument is that Luke repeatedly associated Christians with distinctive Jewish practices in their prayers. For example, a number of Jews associated prayer with fasting and almsgiving as the basic acts of piety. Tobit told Tobias and Raphael: "prayer is good along with fasting, almsgiving, and righteousness."[17] Luke

---

[17]Tob 12:6-10, esp. 8. Cf. also Matt 6:1-18, which associates almsgiving, prayer, and fasting.

associates δεήσεις ("petitions")[18] and προσεύχομαι ("pray")[19] with fasting.[20] He connects δέομαι ("petition")[21] and προσευχή ("prayer")[22] with alms when he relates the conversion of Cornelius. A reader who knows the Jewish world realizes that the paradigmatic Gentile convert is steeped in Jewish piety.

Jews regularly associated places of public worship with prayer. So the synoptic gospels all cite Isa 56:7 in calling the temple "a house of prayer."[23] It is hardly a surprise that in Luke/Acts the temple is the place where one went to pray.[24] The temple was not, however, the only place where one prayed. Acts relates that Paul went out to a προσευχή (proseuche, "place of prayer") in Philippi (Acts 16:13, 16). The term is a often used as a technical term that is equivalent to synagogue.[25] Here it does not appear to denote a structure, but the place where the people regularly worshipped. The association of prayer with worship led some Jews to use the phrase προσκαρτερεῖν τῇ προσευχῇ ("to devote [oneself] to prayer") to designate attendance at Jewish worship assemblies. A first century CE inscription from Kerch near the Black Sea relates the manumission of a slave on the condition that "he devotedly attend the προσευχή with the synagogue of the Jews and the

---

[18]Luke 2:37, Anna; 5:33, where he adds "supplications" to Mark's "fastings" (2:18).

[19]Acts 13:3; 14:23, which both refer to the laying on of hands in the appointment of individuals to offices.

[20]The Didache 8.1-3, gives specific recommendations for Christians to fast (on Wednesdays and Fridays versus Mondays and Thursdays) and to pray (the Lord's Prayer is to be offered three times a day).

[21]Acts 10:2.

[22]Acts 10:4, 31.

[23]Matt 21:13//Mark 11:17/Luke 19:46.

[24]Luke 1:10, the people prayed while Zacharias entered the sanctuary; 18:10, the Pharisee and the tax collector went up to the temple to pray; Acts 3:1, Peter and John went up to the temple at the hour of prayer (see below).

[25]This was the term for a house of worship in Alexandria. Cf. Philo, Flacc. 41, 45, 47, 48, 49, 53, 122; Legat. 132, 134, 137, 138, 148, 152, 156, 157, 165, 191, 346, 371. Cf. also 3 Macc 7:20. Non-Jews also used the term to designate a Jewish place of worship, e.g., Cleomedes, On Circular Motion 2.1.91 (GLAJJ CI.333) and Artemidorus, The Interpretation of Dreams 3.53 (GLAJJ CXV.395).

Godfearers as his guardians."[26] The phrase designates the prayers in the worship rather than the structure. Similarly, Luke depicts the early Jerusalem community as "devoted to prayer" on three occasions.[27] The point is that early Christian worship was similar to Jewish worship.

Early Christians even kept the Jewish afternoon prayer at three. "Peter and John went up to the temple at the ninth hour, the hour of prayer;" this is the same hour when Cornelius prayed.[28] The time was based on the hour when the daily offering (*Tamid*) was offered in the temple.[29] Prayers were by no means limited to specific times or locales. Like their Jewish counterparts, Christians prayed before meals,[30] at farewells,[31] during crises,[32] to make intercessions,[33] and to give thanks.[34] Jews and Christians did not have a monopoly on such prayers: other ethnic groups also prayed during the same occasions.

Finally, there is an unmistakable Jewish cast to the prayers in Luke/Acts. They are largely Jewish in vocabulary and tone. The most explicit are the *Nunc Dimittis* of Simeon which is inspired by Deutero-Isaiah,[35] the prayers of dying Jesus and

---

[26] The inscription is in B. Lifshitz, "Notes d'epigraphie grecque," *RB* 77 (1969) 92-98, esp. 95-96. For a similar inscription see A. Deissmann, *Light from the Ancient East* (reprint ed., Grand Rapids: Baker, 1978) 102 n. 2.

[27] Acts 1:14; 2:42; 6:4. Cf. also Rom 12:12; Col 4:2. On the relationship between the inscriptional evidence and the statements in Acts see T. C. G. Thornton, "'Continuing Stedfast in Prayer'," *Expository Times* 83 (1971) 23-24.

[28] Acts 3:1; 10:30. The references to the sixth hour (i.e., noon) are not to a time devoted to prayer, but presumably to the time when prayer was offered before the mid-day meal (10:9//11:5).

[29] Josephus, *Ant.* 14.65; *m. Pesahim* 5.1.

[30] Luke uses $\epsilon\dot{\upsilon}\lambda o\gamma\dot{\epsilon}\omega$ at Luke 9:16; 24:30 and $\epsilon\dot{\upsilon}\chi\alpha\rho\iota\sigma\tau\dot{\epsilon}\omega$ at Luke 22:17, 19; Acts 27:35. Some have seen a reference to the Lord's Supper in the boat scene of Acts 27:35; however, the scene requires physical sustenance not a worship assembly.

[31] Acts 20:36, Paul and the Ephesian elders; 21:5, Paul and the church at Tyre.

[32] Acts 4:31, for strength after the arrest of Peter and John; 12:5, 12, for Peter when he was imprisoned; 16:25, Paul and Silas in jail at midnight; and 27:29, the ship's crew prayed for daylight.

[33] Luke 22:32, Jesus for Peter; Acts 8:24, Simon asked Peter to pray for him.

[34] Acts 28;15, Paul for the Christians who met him on his way to Rome.

[35] Luke 2:30 from Isa 40:5; Luke 2:31 from Isa 52:10; and Luke 2:32 from Isa 49:6, 9, 13.

Stephen which draw directly from Ps 31:5,[36] and the prayer of the early church after the release of Peter and John which quotes and interprets Psalm 2.[37] I do not want to imply that there are no parallels to prayers in the Greco-Roman world. As we will see, there are. This is essential: Luke was attempting to situate Christianity within the framework of the Greco-Roman world. This demanded literary adaptations to the conventions of that world. At the same time, the ethos of the prayers as a whole is unmistakably Jewish.[38]

Prayer as Perseverance

The attempt to provide a new sense of identity for early Christians was generated by the realization that Christianity had taken its place in history. The distinctive understanding of history is evident in the narrative. Unlike the other gospels which collapsed the story of the church into the story of Jesus, the author of Luke/Acts kept them separate. So, for example, Mark 7:1-23 relates the dissolution of the barrier between Jew and Gentile; Luke/Acts holds this until the conversion of Cornelius in Acts 10:1-11:18. Matthew inserts the word "church" in his gospel with explicit instructions for the church in the second text (16:18; 18:17); Luke/Acts holds it until Acts. Again, John 20:22-23 situates the disciples' reception of the Spirit at a post-resurrection appearance; Luke/Acts delays this until Acts 2:1-4. Mark, Matthew, and John had no alternative but to situate later events in the life of Jesus if they were to narrate them. Luke, on the other hand, could delay them until their appropriate place in the story of the church.

What led to Luke's decision to write a distinct history of the church? While several factors were involved, one of the most important was the delay of the parousia. The earliest levels of tradition in the NT suggest that Christians expected Jesus to return quickly. In the first letter that we have from Paul, the apostle includes himself among those who will be alive at

---

[36]Luke 23:46; Acts 7:59. Ps 31 is a psalm of confidence.

[37]Acts 4:24-30. For a treatment of this text see M.-E. Rosenblatt, "Acts 4:24-30: Prayer of the Friends of Peter and John in Jerusalem," M. Kiley, ed., *Prayer from Alexander to Constantine: A Critical Anthology* (London/New York: Routledge, 1997) 230-34.

[38]Fuhrman, "A Redactional Study of Prayer in the Gospel of Luke," 21-95 and Plymale, *The Prayer Texts of Luke-Acts*, 13-36, have overviews of the possible backgrounds.

the parousia.[39] Mark has the enigmatic statement at the end of the first passion prediction: "I solemnly tell you that there are some standing here who will not taste death before they see the kingdom of God come with power."[40] Matthew's gospel includes the saying that Albert Schweitzer made famous in his study of the historical Jesus: "When they hound you in this city, flee to the next. I solemnly tell you that you will not complete the cities of Israel before the Son of Man comes."[41] The delay forced early Christians to develop theologies that incorporated the absence of the Lord. Paul made the most of the tension with his "already–not yet" eschatological perspective. Mark tempered apocalyptic expectations, but held to them firmly. Matthew began moving in the direction of salvation history, but did not develop a framework that differed from Mark's apocalyptic structure. John knew the apocalyptic tradition, but imposed a realized eschatological perspective on it.

Luke differs from these other authors by openly challenging the apocalyptic tradition on at least two occasions. In one of his editorial introductions, the third evangelist set out his interpretation of the parable that followed: "While they were listening to these things, he added a parable because he was near Jerusalem and they thought that the kingdom of God was about to appear immediately."[42] Luke knew the apocalyptic tradition of early Christians and rejected it. While few if any today would agree with Hans Conzelmann that the delay of the parousia was the central factor that generated Luke/Acts, it would be wrong to disagree with his statement about this text: "Luke is aware that he is contradicting a part of the Christian tradition."[43] The evangelist makes the same challenge in the opening scene of Acts. He articulates the view he wants to discount by presenting it as a question of the disciples: "Lord are you going to restore the kingdom to Israel at this time?" Jesus refused the suggestion: "It is not for you to know the times or the fixed

---

[39] 1 Thess 4:17. Cf. also 1 Cor 7:26, 29.

[40] Mark 9:1. The unit is 8:27-9:1.

[41] Matt 10:23.

[42] Luke 19:11.

[43] H. Conzelmann, *The Theology of St. Luke* (New York: Harper & Row, 1961) 135.

periods that the Father has determined by his own authority."[44] The political nature of the question is bound up with a temporal outlook that the time is now. Both the political and temporal nature of this view are rejected.

Luke replaced the expectation of an imminent parousia with salvation history, i.e., God shapes and controls history for divine purposes. His perspective is evident in numerous texts. The fact that he wrote the history of the church as a separate story from that of Jesus suggests that unlike his apocalyptic predecessors he expected time to extend far into the future. Ernst Käsemann aptly said: "You do not write the history of the church, if you are expecting the end of the world to come any day."[45] This is confirmed by the open-ending of Acts. While there are probably several reasons for this, one of them is that the author wants us to realize that the story of the church is not over: it is ongoing. This is quite different from an apocalyptic outlook which periodizes history in an effort to locate the present within a fixed temporal line. While Luke held on to a future parousia, he did not posit any fixed periods that determine when the end will come. This is why he redacted statements of Q and of Mark to reflect a durative outlook. So, for example, in contrast to the Matthean version of the Lord's Prayer (Q), "give us today our daily bread," Luke has "*give* us our daily bread *daily*." There are two differences: Luke has replaced the aorist "give" ($\delta \acute{o} \varsigma$) with a present "give" ($\delta \acute{\iota} \delta o \upsilon$) which suggests repeated giving. He has made this explicit with the substitution of "daily" ($\tau \grave{o} \quad \kappa \alpha \theta$' $\dot{\eta} \mu \acute{\epsilon} \rho \alpha \nu$) for "today" ($\sigma \acute{\eta} \mu \epsilon \rho o \nu$).[46] He redacted the famous call to discipleship in Mark in a similar way. Mark has: "If any one wants to follow after me, let him deny himself, take up his cross, and follow me." Luke rewrote this as: "If any one wants to come after me, let him deny himself, take up his cross *daily* ($\kappa \alpha \theta$' $\dot{\eta} \mu \acute{\epsilon} \rho \alpha \nu$), and follow me."[47]

The long view of time created problems for disciples. It is one thing to think of being a disciple of Jesus for a brief

---

[44]Acts 1:6-7. Cf. also Luke 24:21.

[45]E. Käsemann, "The Problem of the Historical Jesus," *Essays on New Testament Themes* (Philadelphia: Fortress, 1982) 28.

[46]Matt 6:11//Luke 11:3.

[47]Mark 8:34//Luke 9:23.

period while awaiting the return of the risen Lord, it is another to think of discipleship in terms of a natural lifetime. It is easier to sustain enthusiasm for a brief period than it is for an extended period. Luke was aware of this: he worried that Christians would lose heart and apostacize as they struggled to maintain their faith over their lifetimes. The antidote that he offered was prayer. There are three major texts that make this explicit. The first is the parable of the friend in need (Luke 11:5-8), a parable only attested by Luke. The parable is the middle unit of the first "manual" on prayer. It is sandwiched between two Q texts: the Lord's Prayer and the need to ask.[48] The parable relates the dilemma of a man who is comfortably situated in bed but is awakened by a friend who needs to borrow food for some travelers who have arrived late. The focus of the parable as we have it is on the person in bed.[49] However, Luke's juxtaposition of the parable with the following statements, e.g., "Ask and it will be given to you; seek and you will find; knock and it will be opened to you," changes the focus from the one in bed to the one who is standing at the door knocking. Luke is encouraging Christians to pray as persistently as the man who is out looking for food in the middle of the night.

The second text is a parallel parable: the unjust judge. It opens the second Lukan block of teaching on prayer.[50] The parable tells the story of a widow who will not take no for an answer from an unscrupulous judge who finally agrees to hear her as a means of getting rid of her. The parable is a fascinating example of how a parable of Jesus changed meanings as it moved through different historical contexts. The evangelist offers his interpretation of the parable in the introduction: "he told them a parable so that they would always pray and not give up." The statement is directly linked to eschatological expectations in the context: the disciples are to pray during the delay of the parousia. The preceding material is Jesus' response to the Pharisees about the coming of the kingdom (17:20-21) and his instructions to the disciples about the coming of the Son

---

[48]Matt 6:9-13//Luke 11:2-4 and Matt 7:7-11//Luke 11:9-13. The first two statements in the last unit have a parallel in *The Gospel of Thomas* (Matt 7:7-8//Luke 11:9-10//*Gos. Thom.* 92, 94).

[49]Note especially vv. 5 and 8.

[50]Luke 18:1-13.

of Man (17:22-37). The final saying attached to our parable makes the eschatological dimension explicit: "But will the Son of Man find faith on the earth when he comes?" (18:8). The evangelist realizes that the delay of the parousia created a problem for disciples. His answer was to urge them to pray and to pray with the same persistance that the widow demonstrated in the parable. It may be some time before the Son of Man comes. An earlier and different interpretive tradition focused on the judge. Someone worried about the parallel between the judge and God, i.e., how could an unjust judge represent God? This spawned the interpretation in vv. 6-8a which moves *a minore ad majus*, i.e., if an unjust judge hears the widow, then God will surely hear disciples who are in distress. The original parable (vv. 2-5) probably focused on the unlikely reversal: an unscrupulous judge who enjoyed great power and prestige was overcome by a poor, destitute widow who had no power or prestige. These three interpretations all stem from the same story. The difference is in the focal point for the interpretation. For Jesus it was the interaction between the judge and widow, for an early Christian it was the judge, for Luke it was the widow. The last two parallel the two foci in the parable of the friend in need (the judge//the one in bed and the widow//the one knocking). In both parables, Luke places the emphasis on the need to perservere in prayer.

The same point is made in the Gethsemane scene. Luke rewrites the Markan scene with the emphasis on the struggle the disciples will face. Where Mark has Jesus say to the disciples, "Stay here while I pray," Luke has, "Pray that you do not enter temptation."[51] The disciples are to pray because they face the danger of apostasy. Unfortunately, they find the test more than they can handle. Luke makes this clear by transferring the distress that Jesus feels in Mark to the disciples who are so worn out by it that they can not stay awake.[52] The solution is a repetition of the first exhortation, "Get up and pray that you do not enter into temptation."[53] The inclusio that brackets the failure of

---

[51]Mark 14:32//Luke 22:40.

[52]Luke omits Mark 14:33-34 which relates Jesus' struggle. Later he adds a clause (in italics) which indicates the transfer: "When he got up from his prayer he came to the disciples and found them sleeping *because of grief*" (Mark 14:37//Luke 22:45).

[53]Mark 14:38//Luke 22:46.

the disciples makes the point dramatically: prayer is the means for maintaining vigilance.

These three texts demonstrate that Luke considers prayer the antidote for apostacy. The first two come from the two manuals on prayer. The third represents one of the most dramatic scenes in the gospel where the disciples are in a crisis and need to know how to respond. It is worth remembering that the final petition of the *Pater noster* in Luke is "lead us not into temptation." The power of prayer to help is why Luke presents the Jerusalem community as "devoted to prayer" in three different texts.[54] This is the Christian ideal. While there are other reasons why one might be commanded to pray,[55] the thrust of the Lukan perspective on prayer and eschatology is expressed in the third evangelist's unique conclusion at the end of the eschatological discourse: "Be alert and pray at all times that you may be strong enough to escape all these things that will occur and to stand before the Son of Man."[56]

Prayer and Perception

One of the most fascinating features of Luke's understanding of salvation history is that he links a Deuteronomistic view of history with a Hellenistic view of divine control. The former governs the understanding of God and provides a basis for the author's view that God acts in history. The latter provides an intellectual framework to understand the control that God exercises over history.[57] So Luke can speak of "the plan of God" ($\dot{\eta}$ $\beta ov\lambda\dot{\eta}$ $\tau o\hat{v}$ $\theta\epsilon o\hat{v}$)[58] or "the will of God" ($\tau\dot{o}$ $\theta\acute{\epsilon}\lambda\eta\mu a$ $\tau o\hat{v}$ $\theta\epsilon o\hat{v}$).[59] The phrases refer to the plan by which God governs the

---

[54]Acts 1:14; 2:42; 6:4.

[55]Luke 6:28, pray for those who persecute you; 10:2, pray for laborers; Acts 8:22, Peter commanded Simon to pray for repentance; 8:24, Simon requested Peter to pray for him.

[56]Luke 21:36. Cf. vv. 34-36. The eschatological discourse is Matt 24:1-25:46//Mark 13:1-37//Luke 21:1-36.

[57]The most important treatment of this is J. T. Squires, *The Plan of God in Luke-Acts* (SNTSMS 76; Cambridge: Cambridge University Press, 1993).

[58]Luke 7:30; Acts 2:23; 13:36; 20:27 where the phrase appears and Acts 4:28; 5:38, where the full phrase does not appear but is meant. $Bov\lambda\dot{\eta}$ can also be used of a human plan (Luke 23:51; Acts 27:12, 42).

[59]The exact phrase does not appear, but the concept does in Luke 22:42; Acts 21:14; 22:14. $\theta\acute{\epsilon}\lambda\eta\mu a$ can be used for human will as well (Luke 12:47; 23:25).

course of history. Luke regularly says that something must ($\delta\epsilon\hat{\iota}$) happen. By "must" he means that it is in keeping with God's plan.[60] He uses other verbs less frequently but in the same way: "set" ($\tau\acute{\iota}\theta\eta\mu\iota$),[61] "assign" ($\tau\acute{\alpha}\sigma\sigma\omega$),[62] and "determine" ($\acute{o}\rho\acute{\iota}\zeta\omega$).[63] The plan was foreknown by God. So the large number of words that begin with $\pi\rho o$- underscore the point that God has determined things in advance: "foreknowledge" ($\pi\rho o\gamma\nu$-$\hat{\omega}\sigma\iota\varsigma$),[64] "foretell" ($\pi\rho o\epsilon\hat{\iota}\pi o\nu$),[65] "announce beforehand" ($\pi\rho o\kappa\alpha\tau\alpha\gamma\gamma\acute{\epsilon}\lambda\lambda\omega$),[66] "foresee" ($\pi\rho o o\rho\acute{\alpha}\omega$),[67] "predetermine" ($\pi\rho o o\rho\acute{\iota}\zeta\omega$),[68] "appoint beforehand" ($\pi\rho o\chi\epsilon\iota\rho\acute{\iota}\zeta o\mu\alpha\iota$),[69] and "select beforehand" ($\pi\rho o\chi\epsilon\iota\rho o\tau o\nu\acute{\epsilon}\omega$).[70] The prophets foretold the events of this plan. For this reason the text stresses the fulfillment of Scripture or of the divine will. The most important verbs are "fulfill" ($\pi\lambda\eta\rho\acute{o}\omega$)[71] and "accomplish" ($\tau\epsilon\lambda\acute{\epsilon}\omega$).[72]

Does this mean that humans have no agency in the divine plan? Not at all. Like most biblical authors, Luke affirms divine sovereignty and human freedom simultaneously without attempting to explain the relation between the two as Hellenistic philosophers and later Christians did by drawing a distinction between levels of causation. The starkest formulation of this enigma is the charge leveled against those who demanded Jesus' crucifixion: "this one, handed over by the predetermined plan

---

[60]The impersonal verb is used in this way in Luke 2:49; 4:43; 9:22; 13:33; 17:25; 21:9; 22:37; 24:7, 26, 44; Acts 3:21; 4:12; 9:16; 14:22; 17:3; 19:21; 23:11; 25:10; 27:24, 26. There are other occurrences that refer to a moral obligation.

[61]So used in Acts 1:7; 13:47; 19:21; 20:28.

[62]So used in Acts 13:48; 22:10.

[63]So used in Luke 22:22; Acts 2:23; 10:42; 17:26, 31.

[64]Acts 2:23.

[65]Acts 1:16.

[66]Acts 3:18; 7:52.

[67]Acts 2:31.

[68]Acts 4:28.

[69]Acts 3:20; 22:14; 26:16.

[70]Acts 10:41.

[71]Luke 4:21; 9:31; 21:24; 22:16; 24:44; Acts 1:16; 3:18; 13:25, 27; 14:26; 19:21.

[72]Luke 12:50; 18:31; 22:37; Acts 13:29.

and foreknowledge of God, you nailed (to the cross) through the hands of the lawless."[73] Divine will and human culpability are juxtaposed without any effort to explain the levels of causation.

How does prayer fit into this conceptual framework? It represents the humans attempt to discover and accept God's plan. One of the most notable features of the Lukan treatment of prayer is his repeated insertions of references to prayer in the life of Jesus. There are seven such references (excluding the prayers of Jesus): only one comes from a source. The first of these occurs at the baptism of Jesus. Mark has: "... and he was baptized in the Jordan by John. And immediately when he came up out of the water he saw the heavens torn apart." Luke rewrote this to "Jesus was baptized and while he was praying heaven opened."[74] Luke is the only evangelist to present Jesus at prayer during his baptism. The next reference follows the healing of the leper, immediately before Jesus has his first confrontation with the religious authorities. Mark has: "...but he was out in the wilderness and people came to him from everywhere." Luke altered this to: "He used to retire in the wilderness and pray."[75] Luke again adds a reference to prayer just before Jesus selected the twelve. The third evangelist expanded Mark's simple "he went up the mountain" to "It happened in those days that he went out to the mountain to pray and he spent the whole night in prayer to God."[76] The same pattern surfaces prior to Peter's confession. Mark has a geographical reference in keeping with the pattern of his passion predictions: "Jesus and his disciples went to the villages of Caesarea Philippi." Luke rewrote this to include a reference to prayer: "It happened while he was alone praying that his disciples met him."[77] After Peter's confession, Jesus was transfigured. Mark's editorial frame reads: "And after six days Jesus took Peter, James, and John and took them up to a high mountain privately." Luke expanded this to include Jesus at prayer: "It happened after these sayings about eight days later

---

[73]Acts 2:23.

[74]Mark 1:9-10//Luke 3:21.

[75]Mark 1:45//Luke 5:16.

[76]Mark 3:13//Luke 6:12.

[77]Mark 8:27//Luke 9:18.

that he took Peter, John, and James and went up to a mountain to pray. It happened that while he was praying ..."[78] The sixth reference is an expansion of Q in the travelogue. Matthew introduced the Lord's prayer with "You should pray in this way." Luke provided a setting: "And it happened when he was in a certain place praying, that when he stopped, one of his disciples said to him, 'Lord, teach us to pray, just as John taught his disiciples.'"[79] The final reference is the scene in Gethsemane. Here Luke has taken over Mark's reference to Jesus' prayer; however, he altered it in several important ways. Instead of Mark's "he fell on the ground and prayed," Luke has "he got down on his knees and prayed."[80] Jesus assumes his normal posture for prayer; he is not distressed.[81] For the same reason, Luke omitted the second prayer in Mark: there was no need for Jesus to pray twice.[82]

The same pattern holds true in Acts. The disciples prayed before the selection of Matthias (1:24), before the seven were appointed (6:6), before the Samaritans received the Holy Spirit (8:15), before the revelation that the Gentiles were acceptable (10:9), before the church at Antioch sent out Saul and Barnabas on the Gentile mission (13:3), and before the appointment of leaders in the churches (14:23). Peter[83] and Paul[84] are both presented as praying before major events in their lives. Several of these prayers are deliberate parallels to the prayers of Jesus in the gospel: Jesus is at prayer when he receives the Spirit as are the early disciples,[85] Jesus prayed before selecting the twelve just as the early disciples did before the selection of Matthias,[86] and

---

[78] Mark 9:2//Luke 9:28-29.

[79] Matt 6:9//Luke 11:1.

[80] Mark 14:35//Luke 22:41.

[81] Luke mentions the posture in Acts 7:60; 9:40; 20;36; 21:5.

[82] Mark 14:39. The text implies that Jesus prayed a third time, but does not say so (v. 41).

[83] Acts 8:15; 9:40; 10:9//11:5.

[84] Acts 9:11; 14:23; 16:25; 20:36; 21:5; 22:17; 28:8.

[85] Luke 3:21//Acts 1:14 and 2:1-4.

[86] Luke 6:12//Acts 1:24-25.

both Jesus and Stephen asked to be received in death.[87] The early church prayed as Jesus did.

Why is prayer mentioned at these junctures? The most obvious common denominator of these references is that the majority are at turning points in the narrative: Jesus at his baptism, just before his first confrontation with the authorities, before the selection of the twelve, before Peter's confession, before the transfiguration, and before his death. The evangelist followed a consistent pattern: Jesus prayed before major crises in his life. The same pattern is true in Acts. Prayer is one of the activities that prepares for the appointment of someone to an office (1;24; 13:3; 14:23). It is also a part of the story when the gospel moved from the Jewish to the Samaritan (8:15) to the Gentile worlds (10:9). Prayer is the means by which humans come to understand or accept the plan of God. Jesus prayed: "but not my will, rather let your will be done" (Luke 22:42). Prayer gives us the capacity to accept God's will over against our own. The early Jerusalem community prayed: "You, Lord, who know the hearts of all, show (us) which of these two you have chosen ..." (Acts 1:24). Prayer clarifies the divine will. Whether we find the strength to accept or the capacity to perceive, prayer enables humans to follow the plan of God.

Such prayers are similar to those of Stoic philosophers who taught that humans should pray to accept what God has determined. Epictetus advised: "Do not seek to have the things that happen, happen as you want; rather want the things that happen as they happen and you will do well."[88] The reason for this advice is that God controls all. In the famous *Hymn to Zeus*, Cleanthes wrote:

> Nothing on earth occurs without you, God:
> not in the ethereal divine vault nor in the sea,
> but only whatever evil people do in their foolishness.
> But you are able to make the crooked straight
> and to bring order to disorder. The unloved is lovable
> to you.

---

[87]Luke 23:46; Acts 7:59.

[88]Epictetus, *Encheiridion* 8.

For you have forged all things into one, the good with
the bad,
so that one, eternal, rational order of all things may
come into existence.[89]

Since God controls all, we need to bend our wills to the divine.
Epictetus offered the following prayer as a model:

Lead me, Zeus and you also, Destiny,
wherever I have long ago been assigned by you.
I will follow without hesitation. But if I lack the will
in a state of evil, nonetheless I will follow.[90]

For a Stoic "whatever (God) wills, (the wise) also wills; whatever (God) does not will, this he does not will. How can this be?
How other than by observing the preferences and administration
of God?"[91]

Luke shares this basic outlook; however, he gives it a
distinctive Christian twist. The divine will can be disclosed in a
number of ways. Sometimes God assumes the initiative by
sending an angel,[92] granting a vision,[93] communicating through a
prophet[94] or the Spirit.[95] Such occasions do not require prayer,
although prayer can prepare an individual to receive a special
revelation.[96] On occasions when God does not assume the
initiative, humans pray in an effort to accept or understand the
divine will. It is for this reason that Luke makes the Holy Spirit

---

[89]Ll. 15-21. Translation from the edition of A. A. Long and D. N. Sedley, *Hellenistic Philosophers*, 2 vols. (New York: Cambridge University Press, 1987) 2:326-327.

[90]Epictetus, *Encheiridion* 53.1.

[91]Epictetus, *Diss*. 4.1.99-100.

[92]Luke 1:11-20, 26-38; 2:9-14; Acts 5:19-21; 7:30, 35, 38, 53; 8:26; 10:3-6, 22; 11:1312:7-10, 11; 23:9; 27:23-24.

[93]ὅραμα: Acts 7:31; 9:10-16; 10:3-6, 10-16; 11:5; 12:9; 16:9-10; 18:9-10.

[94]E.g., Luke 1:70; 3:4; 4:17; 18:31; 24:25, 27, 44; Acts 2:16, 30; 3:18, 21, 24; 8:34; 10:43; 11:27; 13:40; 15:15; 21:10; 26:22-27; 28:23, 25.

[95]E.g., Acts 16:6-7; 20:23; 21:4, 11.

[96]It serves as preparation for an ἔκστασις in Acts 10:9 (10-16//11:5-10) and 22:17 (17-21).

83

the answer to prayer. He redacted the statement in Q about "asking" to reflect his special concern. Matthew has: "If you, then, who are evil know to give good gifts to your children, how much more will your heavenly Father give *good things* to those who ask him." Luke rewrote this to: "If you, then, who are evil know to give good gifts to your children, how much more will your heavenly Father give *the Holy Spirit* to those who ask him."[97] Acts contains a dramatic rehearsal of this when Peter and John return to the community after their initial arrest. Luke records a prayer and then says: "When they had finished their petition, the place in which they had gathered was shaken. They were all filled with the Holy Spirit and spoke the word of God with boldness."[98] Prayer is the place where humans open themselves up to the dynamic energy of God's Spirit.[99] We pray in order to open ourselves up to the guidance of the Spirit who enables us to understand God's plan.

Conclusion

I have suggested that prayer is not one dimensional in Luke/Acts, but multi-dimensional. The expansive nature of prayer is not a result of an opaque understanding of prayer on the part of the author that led him to use it loosely. Rather it is a direct consequence of the conviction prayer is an essential element in the fulfillment of God's plan. It is the human acceptance of the divine will. For this reason the evangelist used it in his development of a Christian self-definition. One of the essential components of this definition is that Christianity is a continuation of Israel. This required some attention to prayer. Just as it would have been impossible to think of Judaism with

---

[97]Matt 7:11//Luke 11:13.

[98]Acts 4:31. Cf. vv. 24-30 for the prayer.

[99]See also Acts 8:15-17. The prayer in Acts 1:14 may be understood to be for the promise of the Father (2:1-4). Marcion has a well-known variant in the Lord's Prayer in Luke 11:2 ("may your Holy Spirit come on us and cleanse us"). For a more detailed treatment of the relationship between prayer and the Spirit see G. W. H. Lampe, "The Holy Spirit in the Writings of St. Luke," *Studies in the Gospels: Essays in Memory of R. H. Lightfoot* (Oxford: Oxford University Press, 1955) 169-70. S. S. Smalley, "Spirit, Kingdom and Prayer in Luke-Acts," *NovT* 15 (1973) 59-71, attempts to build on this by suggesting that the triad Spirit, kingdom, and prayer are all interwoven. However, it should be pointed out that the three are not explicitly linked by Luke.

its houses of prayer, assemblies devoted to prayer, times of prayer, and liturgically formed prayers without associating Jews with prayer, so it should have been impossible to think of Christians without also associating them with prayer. Christianity had, however, become something different. The evangelist explained the break with contemporary Judaism by positing salvation history: God planned for this development and attested its progress. This, however, required a longer view of history than Luke's predecessors had acknowledged. The shift in perspective required new strategies for discipleship. Prayer enabled disciples to face the long view of history. It also made it possible for them to understand the place of Christianity in history and to accept their role within it.

As one who lives almost two millenia after the events that Luke narrates, I am grateful that his work made its way into the New Testament. It not only offered readers at the end of the first century an understanding of Christianity that made sense of the radical changes that had occurred within the century, but provides us with an interpretation of history that embraces the march of time. It not only supplied ancient disciples a means to endure and to understand an uncertain future, it suggests that we can persevere and play our part in the unfolding of God's plan. We do so in the same way as our first century counterparts, we get down on our knees.

Appendix

The terms that Luke uses for prayer and their frequencies are:[100] αἰτέω ("ask") Luke, 5 times (11 times total)[101] and Acts, 0 times (10 times total)[102] versus Mark, 1 time (9 times total)[103] and Matthew, 9 times (14 times total);[104] ἀνθομολογέομαι ("praise") Luke, 1 time as a hapax legomenon in the NT;[105] βοάω ("cry out") Luke, 1 time (4 times total) but never elsewhere for prayer in the Synoptics or Acts;[106] δέομαι ("petition") Luke, 3 times (8 times total)[107] and Acts, 4 times (7 times total)[108] versus Mark, 0 times and 1 time in Matthew[109] and δέησι´ ("petition") Luke, 3 times[110] and not at all in Mark and Matthew; ἐξομολογέομαι ("praise") Luke, 1 time (2 times total)[111] and Matthew, 1 time (2 times total) and nowhere else in the Synoptics and Acts for prayer;[112]

---

[100]For a detailed treatment of the Lukan terms see O. G. Harris, "Prayer in Luke-Acts: A Study of the Theology of Luke," (Ph.D. diss., Vanderbilt, 1966) 7-22; Monloubou, *La prière selon Saint Luc*, 91-167; and C. M. Fuhrman, "A Redactional Study of Prayer in the Gospel of Luke" (Ph.D. diss., Southern Baptist Theological Seminary, 1981) 1-7. I have only provided statistics for the Synoptic Gospels, although the same point can be made with reference to the fourth gospel.

[101]Luke 11:9, 10, 11, 12, 13. Cf. also 1:63; 6:30; 12:48; 23:23, 35, 52, where it is not used for prayer.

[102]Cf. Acts 3:2, 14; 7:46; 9:2; 12:20; 13:21, 28; 16:29; 25:3, 15, where it is not used for prayer.

[103]Mark 11:24. Cf. also 6:22, 23, 24, 25; 10:35, 38; 15:8, 43, where it is not used for prayer.

[104]Matt 6:8; 7:7, 8, 9, 10, 11; 18:19; 21:22. Cf. also 5;42; 14:7; 20:20, 22; 27:20, where it is not used for prayer.

[105]Luke 2:38.

[106]Luke 18:7. Cf. Luke 3:4; 9:38; 18:38; Acts 8:7; 17:6; 25:24, where it is not used for prayer. It appears in Matt 3:3; 27:46 and Mark 1:3; 15:34, but not in reference to prayer.

[107]Luke 10:2; 21:36; 22:32. Cf. also 5:12; 8:28, 38; 9:38, 40 where it is not used for prayer.

[108]Acts 4:31; 8:22, 24; 10:2. Cf. also 8:34; 21:39; 26:3 where it is not used for prayer.

[109]Matt 9:38.

[110]Luke 1:13; 2:37; 5:33. It does not appear in Acts.

[111]Luke 10:21. Cf. also Luke 22:6; Acts 19:18, where it does not refer to prayer.

ἐπικαλέω ("call upon") Acts 1 time and nowhere in the Synoptics;[113] εὐλογέω ("bless") Luke, 4 times (13 times total)[114] versus Mark, 3 times (5 times total)[115] and Matthew, 2 times (5 times total);[116] εὐχαριστέω ("give thanks") Luke, 3 times (4 times total)[117] and Acts, 2 times[118] versus Mark, 2 times[119] and Matthew, 2 times;[120] εὔχομαι ("wish") Acts, 2 times[121] and nowhere in the Synoptic gospels; ζητέω ("seek") Luke, 2 times (25 times total)[122] and Matthew, 2 times (14 times total)[123] and not in Mark or Acts for prayer;[124] κράζω ("cry") Acts, 1 time (11 times total)[125] and only Matthew, 1 time (12 times total) in the Synoptic Gospels;[126] κρούω ("knock") Luke, 2 times (4 times

---

[112]Matt 11:25. Cf. also 3:6 and Mark 1:5, where it does not refer to prayer.

[113]Acts 7:59. Cf. also Acts 1:23; 2:21; 4:36; 9:14, 21:10:5, 18, 32; 11:13; 12:12, 25; 15:17; 22:16; 25:11, 12, 21, 25; 26:32; 28:19, where it does not refer to prayer. I take the expression "call on his name" to refer to confession and loyalty, although this does not exclude prayer (Acts 2:21; 9:14, 2122:16. Cf. also 15:17. It only appears once in the Synoptic Gospels, Matt 10:25.

[114]Luke 2:28 (29-32); 9:16; 24:30; 24:53. Cf. also 1:28, 42, 64 (?); 2:34; 6:28; 13:35; 19:38; and Acts 3:25, 26 where it does not refer to prayer.

[115]Mark 6:41; 8:7; 14:22. Cf. also 11:9. 10 where it does not refer to prayer.

[116]Matthew 14:19; 26:26. Cf. also 21:9; 23:39; 25:34 where it does not refer to prayer.

[117]Luke 18:11; 22:17, 19. Cf. also Luke 17:16 where it does not refer to prayer.

[118]Acts 27:35; 28:15.

[119]Mark 8:6; 14:23.

[120]Matthew 15:36; 26:27.

[121]Acts 26:29; 27:29

[122]Luke 11:9, 10. Cf. also 2:48, 49; 5:18; 6:19; 9:9; 11:16, 24, 29; 12:29, 31, 48; 13:6, 7, 24; 15:8; 17:33; 19:3, 10, 47; 20:19; 22:2, 6; 24:5, where it does not refer to prayer.

[123]Matt 7:7, 8. Cf.also 2:13, 20; 6:33; 12:43, 46, 47; 13:45; 18:12; 21:46; 26:16, 59; 28:5.

[124]The closest possibility is Acts 17:27, which might include prayer but is not restricted to it.

[125]Acts 7:60. Cf. also Luke 4;41; 9:39; 18:39; 19:40; Acts 7:57; 14:14; 16:17; 19:28, 32, 34; 21:28, 36; 23:6; 24:21, where it does not refer to prayer.

[126]Matthew 27:50. Cf. also 8:29; 9:27; 14:26, 30; 15:22, 23; 20:30, 31; 21:9, 15; 27:23, where it does not refer to prayer. Mark uses it, but not in reference to prayer: 3:11; 5:5, 7; 9:24, 26; 10:47, 48; 11:9; 15:13, 14.

total) and Acts, 0 times (2 times total)[127] as well as Matthew, 2 times[128] and nowhere in Mark; προσεύχομαι ("pray") Luke, 19 times[129] and Acts, 16 times[130] versus Mark, 10 times[131] and Matthew, 16 times[132] and προσευχή ("prayer") Luke, 3 times[133] and Acts, 9 times[134] versus Mark, 2 times[135] and Matthew, 3 times[136] This means that the Gospel of Luke has used twelve verbs and nouns for prayer, Acts, seven, Mark, five of these, and Matthew, ten of them.[137] Luke/Acts together has fifteen different words or cognates for prayer. Luke refers to prayer 47 times in the gospel and 35 times in Acts, whereas Mark has 18 references (62% less than the gospel of Luke) and Matthew, 39 (17% less than the gospel of Luke). The order of vocabulary and frequency from the highest to the lowest is therefore Luke, Matthew, Acts, Mark.

---

[127]Luke 11:9, 10. Cf. also 12:36; 13:25; Acts 12:13, 16, where it does not refer to prayer; although Luke 13:25 refers to an appeal to the Lord at judgment.

[128]Matt 7:7,8.

[129]Luke 1:10; 3:21; 5:16; 6:12, 28; 9:18, 28, 29; 11:1 (*bis*), 2; 18:1, 10, 11; 20:47; 22:40, 41, 44, 46.

[130]Acts 1:24; 6:6; 8:15; 9:11, 40; 10:9, 30; 11:5; 12:12; 13:3; 14:23; 16:25; 20:36; 21:5; 22:17; 28:8.

[131]Mark 1:35; 6:46; 11:24, 25; 12:40; 13:18; 14:32, 35, 38, 39.

[132]Matt 5:44; 6:5 (*bis*), 6 (*bis*), 7, 9; 14:23; 19:13; 23:14; 24:20; 26:36, 39, 41, 42, 44.

[133]Luke 6:12; 19:46; 22:45.

[134]Acts 1:14; 2:42; 3:1; 6:4; 10:4, 31; 12:5; 16:13, 16.

[135]Mark 9:29; 11:17.

[136]Matt 17:21; 21:13, 22.

[137]A complete analysis would require carefully working through both Mark and Matthew to make sure that they do not use any additional words for prayer.

Chapter Five
We Will Pray: Preaching About Prayer in Luke/Acts

Introduction

There is at least one thing that Luke's original audience has in common with the modern church–they did not witness the events described in Luke/Acts. They did not walk with Jesus, hear him teach or see the miracles he performed. They did not see the risen Christ nor witness the exciting events of those early years of the church. Like us, they were dependent upon the "eyewitnesses" Luke used to reconstruct the ministry of Jesus and the early church. Yet they, like the first disciples, and we were called to be God's witnesses in the world, proclaiming the gospel of Jesus Christ "to the ends of the earth" (Acts 1:8). We often wonder, as they must have, how we can possibly make the kind of impact in the world around us that those first disciples did. How will we overcome the doubt and despair that often beset us? And how will we find the strength to persevere to the end and pass on this faith to the next generation? Luke's answer appears to be quite simple. We will find the strength to face temptation and sustain us through trials the way Jesus and his first disciples did–we will pray.

Now that may seem like a rather simplistic response, especially in our technologically advanced and enlightened culture, but that is precisely the perspective that infuses both the account of Jesus' ministry and the account of how those first disciples followed his example. No other gospel has such an emphasis upon the Holy Spirit as the empowering force in the life of Jesus and his disciples as well as on prayer as the vehicle for that encounter. From the prayers of hopeful parents and expectant prophets before the birth of Christ to that gripping scene of Jesus on the Mount of Olives at the end of his life to the prayers of the church for boldness in the face of adversity, prayer permeates this entire account. Luke reminds all who would preach about prayer to the church that just as we share the same commission as those first disciples so we also share the same spiritual resources.

There is no greater expression of our faith than prayer. I'm not just talking about the pious, public prayers we hear in church. Rather I have in mind the prayers that grandmothers say for children whose parents neglect to pray for them; the kinds of prayers that single parents say when they seek the strength to live faithfully for another day; or the prayers ministers say for churches when no one seems to give *them* a prayer. Unlike our modern preoccupation with proficiency in prayer, which often emphasizes techniques and strategies for "success," Luke's concern is persistence in prayer. This is best conveyed by Jesus' haunting question at the conclusion of a parable on prayer– "When the Son of Man comes, will he find faith on the earth?" (Luke 18:8b). The implication is that the same God who calls us together as a church and sends us out into the world will also empower us to fulfill our mission by the power of the Holy Spirit if we will just ask. Luke makes this point quite clear in a familiar passage about prayer in which Jesus compares the nurturing instincts of a flawed ("evil") human father who knows how to give good gifts to his children to God who gives "the Holy Spirit to those who ask him" (Luke 11:13). Indeed, there is no other account in the Bible that has more to say about the power of prayer.

So how does one preach about prayer from Luke/Acts in a way that inspires as well as informs? We begin by recognizing that the prominence of prayer in this account, both in teaching and example, suggests that prayer is one of the keys to properly understanding Luke's portrayal of Jesus and the early history of the church. No serious attempt to preach from Luke or Acts can ignore the influence and emphasis of this theme. There are several approaches that may prove helpful to the preacher to keep that emphasis before the church. The first approach is simply a survey of the way prayer functions in this account. Which means understanding and appreciating the connection between prayer and the Holy Spirit as well as understanding the significance of prayer at some of the most important moments in Jesus' ministry and the ministry of the church. Second, one may observe the various purposes of prayer for the church that become reasons for disciples to pray. Third, the preacher can focus specifically upon Jesus' teaching about prayer, including the parables about prayer that provide a commentary on the relationship that is at work in prayer. Finally, one must pay special attention in Luke/Acts to the function of intercessory prayer. In particular, Jesus' role as intercessor, as well as exemplar, offers the preacher a unique and liberating view both of Jesus and ministry.

A Survey of Prayer

A survey of prayer in Luke/Acts might begin by noting the inherent connection between prayer and the Holy Spirit. Or one could examine the passages that address the place and function of the Holy Spirit to discover that in most of these references prayer is either mentioned or implied. For example, it is when the priest Zechariah is praying that he receives the announcement that his prayers have been answered, and his wife, who has been barren for many years, will bear a son who will be "filled with the Holy Spirit" (Luke 1:10). Likewise, when Jesus is presented at the Temple for the first time in Luke chapter 2, he is recognized as God's Messiah by two elderly righteous people–Anna and Simeon–who had been anticipating this moment of revelation while they waited faithfully, praying and fasting at the Temple for years. It is important to note in these stories the connection between expectation and prayer which is made explicit later in Jesus' teaching about prayer in Luke 11:9-11.

We can also observe the parallel between the baptism of Jesus (Luke 3) and the birth of the church (Acts 2). Both Jesus and the church are praying when the Spirit descends upon them, and as Fred Craddock reminds us, in Luke/Acts both Jesus and the church are born of the Holy Spirit.[1] It is interesting to note Luke's strategy as he speaks of the Holy Spirit and prayer. In the entire gospel of Luke we find neither example of the Holy Spirit at work in Jesus' disciples nor any example of their praying, even though they ask to be taught to pray and are admonished to pray. Yet throughout Acts we find example after

---

[1] Fred Craddock, *Luke*, Interpretation: A Bible Commentary for Preaching and Teaching (Louisville: John Knox Press, 1990), 10.

example of the transforming and empowering work of the Holy Spirit in the church through prayer. Because Luke has the luxury to write about the ministry of Jesus in his gospel and the continuing ministry of Jesus through his disciples in Acts, he can maintain this separation to make his point that the ministry of Jesus does indeed continue in his church. In the early chapters of Acts we read of those first disciples being devoted to prayer (1:12-14), and later we read of the entire church devoted to daily prayer (2:42). In chapter 4 the church, faced with increased opposition and threats, immediately took their concerns to God and sought the power of the Spirit of God to give them boldness to proclaim the gospel. And throughout Acts, with each major decision or event, prayer is essential to its success. It is worth noting that in each of these examples prayer is the first response of the church rather than the last resort. Prayer is also the continuing strategy of the church.

The advantage of this kind of broad approach is to give the church an overall sense of the prominent role of prayer in the life and ministry of Jesus and the early church, which is just another way of seeing that it is God at work and not ourselves. We are too enthralled with our own micro-management of a text, a sermon, a class, or a program sometimes to be able to recognize the sovereignty of God. However, after such an overview it helps to look deeper into the nature and function of prayer, and one of the ways to approach that is to examine the purposes of prayer.

The Purposes of Prayer

In Luke/Acts prayer appears to have at least three purposes, all of them derived from the Holy Spirit. Prayer functions both to nurture the relationship between disciples and God and to invite the Spirit of God to guide, sustain and empower the people of God. It is important when preaching about prayer to a culture that often regards prayer as either self-talk or magic to make a clear distinction between the Spirit of God that is working in the church and prayer as the vehicle for that relationship. On this point the preacher must be clear—the power of prayer is not found in the "poverty of our asking, but according to the richness of (God's) grace."[2] And yet God

---

[2] Reinhold Niebuhr, *Justice and Mercy* (San Francisco: Harper & Row, 1974), 12.

expects us to always be asking and seeking and knocking (Luke 11:9-10). For Luke, the relationship between God and the children of God is not about equality or reciprocity, but it is about community and communication.

Throughout Luke/Acts the Spirit of God is constantly guiding the action. Indeed, one might say that the Holy Spirit functions as the "director" of the action in Acts. At pivotal moments the Spirit is guiding and revealing the will of God to those who seek to know it, and most of those are occasions of prayer. From the very beginning of the gospel when Zechariah is informed that his wife, Elizabeth, will bear a son who will be "filled with the Holy Spirit," it is as an answer to prayer (Luke 1:13). Later, when the baby Jesus is presented at the Temple, the Holy Spirit reveals to two elderly, righteous people–Anna and Simeon–the identity of God's Messiah. Luke notes their expectation and desire for this revelation, as expressed by constant fasting and prayer.

In chapter 9 of Luke we encounter a very different kind of revelation described as the transfiguration of Jesus. Although this event is prominent in all three of the synoptic gospels, Luke gives this event a unique setting. He describes it as occurring while Jesus was praying. In fact, Luke adds that the whole purpose for taking those three disciples–Peter, James and John–to the mountain that day was to pray. And it is while praying that Jesus' glory is revealed, much like the affirmation of the Spirit after his baptism in chapter 3. Noting the selection of those three disciples on this occasion one is immediately reminded of the events in the garden of Gethsemane on the night Jesus was betrayed; except Luke does not mention any disciples being singled out that night. (In fact, Luke's portrayal of the disciples that night is the most sympathetic of all the gospels. More on that later.) Instead, he adds another unique detail to his account of the transfiguration to draw a different kind of connection between these two events. He mentions that the three disciples were "weighed down with sleep," but because they managed to stay awake "they saw his glory" (9:32). "Watch and pray" was Jesus' admonition to his disciples on that last night, reminding us that one of the primary ways to be watchful is to pray. This is particularly striking when one contrasts the revelations in the gospel of Matthew (to Joseph, the magi and Pilate's wife) that all occur in dreams, with the visions of Luke/Acts that all seem to occur when the recipients are awake.

This is even more striking when one compares the conversion stories of Paul and Cornelius which are related in such close proximity in the book of Acts (chapters 9-11). In chapter 9 we read about Paul (then identified as Saul) and his encounter with Jesus on the road from Jerusalem to Damascus. He is fully awake when this encounter occurs, as confirmed by the experience of his traveling companions. But Luke records that "though his eyes were open, he could see nothing" (9:8). For three days he remained this way until God directs a rather skeptical disciple named Ananias to go and heal him of his blindness, both physical and spiritual. Both Saul and Ananias are informed of God's plan in almost simultaneous visions while praying. (In the case of Ananias one may assume this by the context.) In the next chapter we read of the conversion of a Roman centurion named Cornelius by the apostle Peter. Again we find two visions that bring together a somewhat confused and reluctant preacher with someone who is devoutly seeking the will of God, and both of them occur in the midst of prayer.

This makes one wonder if the real "evangelism strategy" for Acts is prayer? Increasingly, many churches that are growing attribute their growth to a renewed commitment to prayer. A friend of mine tells the story of reaching the point early in his ministry when he became convinced that he could no longer continue without ruining his health. So he prayed for God to show him where the open hearts were, and he promised to be faithful to teach them. For decades God has been faithful; he has been obedient, and thousands have been taught.

A second purpose for prayer in Luke/Acts is simply to sustain the church. We see this function of prayer first with Jesus in Luke. On several occasions we are told how Jesus withdrew from the crowds to pray, often all night long. In chapter 21, after exhorting the crowds in Jerusalem not to let the burdens of life weigh them down but to stay awake and pray for the strength to escape the tribulations to come, Jesus takes his own advice and retreats to the Mount of Olives where he spent several nights. It is reasonable to assume, given the way Jesus retreats with his disciples on the last night of his life to pray, that this was what he did every night he spent there.

Often the prayers to sustain the church lead to the

empowering of the church by the Spirit of God in some surprising way. A good example of this is in Acts 12 when the church gathers to fervently pray for Peter who has been arrested by Herod and is in danger of being executed. While the church prays for his protection from harm Peter is visited that night by an angel who leads him out of the prison, past the guards, and back to the house where the church is still praying. Peter knocks on the door and a servant named Rhoda answers it. But she is so surprised to see Peter that she fails to open the door. Instead she runs back to the group that is praying to inform them that Peter is at the door; perhaps so intent in their prayer for Peter's protection they are not prepared for God to give them even more than they asked for. The same thing occurs in the story of Paul and Silas. They were praising God and praying together in a Philippian jail one night when suddenly an earthquake strikes and they have an opportunity to proclaim the gospel to the jailer and his entire family (one would assume the rest of the prisoners as well).

These examples serve to remind us of how often the church does not do great things because we do not ask for the things that only God can do. Too often we are limited by our view of God and our relationship to God as children. Or we are limited by our gradually diminishing expectations that will eventually reduce prayer to a monologue and finally silence.

Jesus' Teaching on Prayer

In chapters 11 and 18 we have the heart of Jesus' teaching about prayer in the gospel of Luke. These chapters are actually part of a larger section in Luke that is often referred to as the travel narrative (9:51-19:44), when Jesus "set his face to go to Jerusalem" (9:51) for the final confrontation. The travel narrative functions as a metaphor for the pilgrimage of faith that all disciples make and offers them the kind of spiritual equipping they will need to complete the journey.[3] Chapter 11 begins with a request from his disciples to teach them to pray. What follows is what we traditionally refer to as "the Lord's prayer," although Luke's version is somewhat abbreviated from the one in Matthew (Matthew 6:9-13) and does not share the same concerns. In Matthew the concern of Jesus seems to focus

---

[3] Charles Talbert, *Reading Luke: A Literary and Theological Commentary on the Third Gospel* (New York: Crossroad, 1982), 111-113.

on how to pray (Matthew 6:9), as well as how not to pray. In Luke's account the concern is simply that disciples learn to pray (11:1) and that they "should always pray and not give up" (18:1).

Preachers would do well to pay attention here. Too often it is assumed that what the church needs is constant critiques and warnings about the way it prays without recognizing an even greater need to be encouraged to pray. Ironically, this imbalance could result in promoting such attention to proper technique and content in prayer (especially in public prayer) that it might actually serve to discourage others from attempting to pray, thus violating the very spirit of what Jesus was teaching in Matthew 6.

In contrast, Jesus' model for prayer in Luke 11 is followed by a story about a friend who comes at midnight seeking bread for a guest who has arrived unexpectedly. Scholars disagree over whether the focus of this story is on the one who arises and fulfills his friend's request out of a sense of duty or on the friend who refuses to be denied. Regardless of which character one chooses to emphasize as the interpretive key to this story, one thing is clear: the request is not granted on the basis of friendship. This sets up a contrast that is expanded a few verses later when Jesus compares the loving instincts of a flawed ("evil") father to the transcendent love of a perfect God.

This same technique is employed in Jesus' story of the persistent widow and the unjust judge in Luke 18. Here Jesus offers the story of a judge who "neither feared God nor respected others" and a widow who has no standing in the community, much less before this judge. And yet, Jesus says, this widow's request was granted by the judge not on the basis of the judge's integrity or the widow's status, but simply because of her refusal to be denied justice. Some have misinterpreted this story, as well as the one in chapter 11, by focusing primarily upon the persistence of the two petitioners, but that is not the point here. Rather, it is the stark contrast between the ones who eventually and grudgingly granted the requests of their persistent, but "undeserving" petitioners and God who freely desires to grant the requests of those who are God's children. In both stories, as in the teaching that surrounds them, the point is that God's children have every reason to pray because of–God's character and because of their standing before

God which is based entirely upon God's character. This offers a certain irony when one considers the next parable.

In a story that contrasts the prayers of an "insider" (a religious leader) and an "outsider" (a tax-collector), Jesus offers another insight as to the nature and purpose of prayer. This time the contrast is not between a petitioner and the one being petitioned, but between two petitioners who stand before God—at least they both appear to be petitioners. While to Jesus' original audience the greatest difference between these two men would have appeared to be their social standing, Jesus focuses on the content of their prayers as a true reflection of their standing before God. The religious leader's prayer appears to be rather normal, not unlike many prayers of thanksgiving in the Psalms where the ones praying rejoice in not being found in the company of the unrighteous. Yet the story unmasks the heart of this man to reveal an attitude toward others that effectively hinders his relationship to God in prayer. While the parables of the friend at midnight and the persistent widow seem to be addressed to those who assume so little of God that seeking God's blessing seems impossible, this one seems to be addressed to those who assume so much about themselves that seeking God's blessing seems unnecessary. The religious leader leaves worship without God's blessing for one simple reason—he doesn't ask for it…because he doesn't believe he needs it.

Churches today are filled with both kinds of people. Some have given up on prayer because they have an image of God that is based upon how they would regard someone like them if they were God. Quite often their image of God is that of an angry, demanding, and unloving parent. Folks like these can never relax in their relationship with God nor can they allow anyone else to be so confident. But far more have given up on prayer without even knowing it. They still say their prayers, but they just do not pray. For when true confession and repentance are considered inappropriate for an "upbeat" worship, gratitude and thanksgiving are reduced to self-congratulations, and what masquerades as forgiveness and healing is really just the all-too-human "power of positive thinking."

Intercessory Prayer

One of the most significant contributions of Luke/Acts to the discussion about prayer is the role of intercessory prayer. In the gospel of Luke Jesus is portrayed as both the exemplar of prayer for disciples ("Lord, teach us to pray…" Luke 11:2) and the intercessor on their behalf. Most of us are quite familiar with Jesus as our example in prayer, but we still have a lot to learn about the image of Jesus as intercessor. One of the things that the Bible tells us about the incarnation is that he came to show us the fullness of God; but too often we view Jesus through our own distorted self-image. Nowhere is that more evident than in our prayers.

One story from the last night of Jesus' life illustrates this point. In Luke 22:31-34 we find the familiar prediction by Jesus that Peter will deny him three times before the dawn of another day. Although Peter vigorously insisted that it would never happen, Jesus assured him that it would. Luke's account of this differs significantly from the one in Matthew and Mark, which is essentially the same. This change is consistent with what has already been noted – that in the gospel of Luke the passion of Jesus is reduced from what is portrayed in Matthew and Mark. However, one might also conclude that Jesus' passion is actually redirected from himself to the compassion of Jesus toward his disciples. In fact, Luke's portrayal of the disciples on that last night is a very sympathetic one. For example, when the disciples fall asleep in the garden Luke attributes it to grief rather than weakness. (In Matthew and Mark, Jesus is the only one who is overwhelmed with grief, and the disciples appear uncaring when they fall asleep.) Jesus' rebuke to the disciples and his admonition that "the spirit is willing, but the flesh is weak" is also absent from Luke's account. Instead we see Jesus admonishing them to "get up and pray that you may not enter into the time of trial" (22:46).

This shift is evident most vividly in Jesus' prediction of Peter's denial according to Luke. First, we notice that the focus is primarily on Peter. And Peter is portrayed as passive rather than active in his denial. "Satan desires to sift all of you like wheat," Jesus says to them, but then he turns to Peter and says something that offers a completely different perspective to this tragic episode, "but I have prayed for you that your own faith will not fail." Set that alongside another addition that Luke makes to the tradition later in that same chapter when, immediately after Peter denies Jesus for the third time he writes, "The Lord turned and looked at Peter" (22:61). Now usually when this moment is conveyed in sermons the look on Jesus is a combination of hurt, anger, and bitter disappointment (heavy on the anger). After all, is not that the way we would feel after such a denial? But this unique contribution to the passion narrative needs to be set in the context of those earlier remarks to Peter if we ever hope to understand what Luke was attempting to express.

A couple of years ago I met a visitor coming out of church who was a student in one of the local universities. I asked him when he was graduating, and he replied that he should have graduated in the spring with his classmates, but he had to take two more classes over the summer before he would obtain his diploma. I lamented with him over this, but he assured me that he felt very fortunate to have the opportunity to graduate at all. It turned out that he was taking these two classes to make up for the credit he had lost when he cheated on an exam the previous semester. "How did they catch you?" I asked him. "They didn't," he replied, "I turned myself in." Anticipating my next question, he said he decided to turn himself in after he went back to his dorm room and remembered something his mother had said when he left for school one year. She hugged him and explained that she knew he would face a lot of temptations while away at school, but she wanted him to remember (as she looked him square in the eye) that she loved him, and she knew that he would always do the right thing. As he sat there alone in his room, thinking about what he had just done and what his mother had said to him, he said, "All I could see was that look on her face and then I knew what I had to do." I didn't ask him, but I cannot imagine there was anything in her look that conveyed condemnation or rejection. Rather, I suspect it was a look of honesty, love, and even pain that brought him to his senses and restored his sense of right and wrong.

I wonder if that's the look Peter saw that day when he remembered the words of Jesus? And I wonder if preachers need to consider more carefully how we convey that scene to disciples who may have imagined all too well the withering glare of Jesus in their direction. (I've often imagined it like those images of melting faces and the laser vision that burns holes through people in a horror movie.) It seems unlikely to me that Luke felt the need to "turn up the heat" on his fellow disciples with this unique contribution to the gospel

101

story. One might even consider this scene as providential, as Jesus "looking out" for Peter. Rather, this seems more like an injection of hope into an otherwise bitter moment. The kind of hope that needs to be part of every sermon we preach and every prayer we pray. After all, Luke recognizes that his readers are probably in for the long haul and need all the hope and encouragement they can get.

Just as there is no greater expression of our faith than prayer, there is no greater expression of our hope than praying for others. Perhaps one of the most overused but potentially most powerful sentiments is, "I will pray for you." I do not know how long it was before I began to keep a personal prayer list, but I started the day I realized how often I promised to pray for others but never did. Grandparents need to be praying for their children and grandchildren. Parents need to be praying for their children, especially when all hope seems lost. Several years ago a friend of mine asked me what I would do differently in raising one of my children who was adopted. I thought about all the mistakes I had made in raising him; all the advice my wife and I had received over the years; all the guilt and anger we sometimes felt as a result. I remember how often we thought that no one else knew what we were going through. No one else knew our son and loved him the way we did. No one else had invested more or sacrificed more for his future. And then I realized that there was someone who knew what we were going through. Someone who knew our pain and anger and who invested more and sacrificed more for our son because this person loved him more than we did. It was God. I related that story in a church bulletin a few weeks later, and about two years later when we were celebrating the graduation of several high school seniors from our church I commented to several parents on the almost miraculous changes in their children in the last year. Every one of them responded that they had put that article on the refrigerator that day and began praying for their children every day. "Don't praise us," they said, "praise God."

Conclusion

Finally, we must not overlook the importance of the preacher's personal prayer life in any attempt to preach about prayer. Preaching about prayer without the personal experience of an active prayer life is like showing the slides from someone else's vacation. The truth is, like faith itself, not everything that can be learned about prayer comes from scripture–some of it must be learned in the experience of actually praying. That is particularly true when one is preaching about prayer from Luke/Acts. In his book *The Witness of Preaching*, Tom Long offers three traditional models for preachers–the herald, the pastor and the storyteller.[4] Then he offers his own model–the preacher as "witness," not as an addition to the list, but as the metaphor that best captures what authentic preaching is all about.[5] For the preacher as witness speaks not just from the authority of scripture, but also from the authority of personal experience. Only then can we truly join the "cloud of witnesses" that "cannot but speak the things which we have seen and heard" (Acts 4:20).

---

[4] Thomas Long, *The Witness of Preaching* (Louisville: Westminster John Knox Press, 1989), 24.

[5] Ibid., 41.

Part II

Sermons from Luke/Acts

HEALING OUR OWN PARALYSIS

One of the great challenges the preacher faces with many of the stories in the Gospels is the "been there, done that" expectation of our audiences. How does one take a familiar story such as the healing of the paralytic and, in Craddock's words, preach so that the audience hears "as though for the first time." When I lived in Temple, Texas, I was blessed by the presence of the LeFan family. James and Jackie have ministered to the Western Hills church for almost fifty years; James served as the preaching minister there for 39 years. Their son Mike has been a living testimony of faith in the community for all of those years. His circumstances made this remarkable text come alive for me, and I have endeavored to share that journey with the audience.

At the same time, the heart of this story, like so many in the Gospels, is not about physical healing but the greater good of human healing—transforming our humanity back into the image of God. Thus, the ultimate focus in the sermon is the announcement that Jesus is indeed the one who can forgive sins.

Chapter Six
Sermons from Luke

JOHN O. YORK

HEALING OUR OWN PARALYSIS
TEXT: LUKE 5:17-26

When James and Jackie's first-born son came into the world, he was as healthy and wonderful as the proud parents dreamed and prayed he would be. The apple of his dad's eye. The first eight years of his life, in fact, were all wonderful, healthy, normal growing–up years. But then when Mike was eight, he contracted polio. For months he hung on the edge of life in a Houston, Texas hospital. When he was finally able to go home again, he was paralyzed from the neck down to his feet, and he required an iron lung in order to receive enough oxygen for life. No one looked to the preacher father or to the mother or to the son and said, "Who sinned, this boy or his parents?" It was just a tragedy of life. The question was, what would the quality of life be for little Mike from then on? Fortunately, Mike had wonderfully supportive parents and friends, and he lived at a time when medical technology was making rapid advances. He got to where he could be out of the iron lung for several hours at a time. The medical community also kept inventing more portable equipment and bed-type wheel chairs to improve his mobility. Mike's story is really remarkable in the end. Mike's toes have done incredible things over the years. First using typewriters and then computers, Mike not only got a high school education, he graduated from college. He is an accomplished author and artist, a prolific writer with free lance articles in a number of different magazines, and a few years ago he even published a book about his own life. He's a ham radio operator and for several years served as president of the local club where he lives. Mike and his parents are indeed remarkable people.

Mike is fortunate to live today, when handicapped people are considered valuable assets to society, when they can have a chance to live productive, reasonably whole lives. In the first century, Mike probably would not have lived to begin with, but had he survived as a paralytic, he would have experienced all of the prejudice and rejection that other humans can sometimes heap upon those whom they no longer consider to be real people. In the first century, any physical ailment that left you immobilized and unable to work, whether it was blindness or paralysis–any kind of crippling disorder that made one abnormal–also made you a non-person. That is why it is common in the Gospels to read the words "blind" and "beggar" together. At whatever age, such a disease or disability left one at the mercies of other people. You became a non-person, socially and religiously. A paralyzed person could not participate in the Jewish religious life at all because he was unclean. He could offer no sacrifice, he could not participate in the feasts. He was outside the religious and social boundaries. Obviously there were no wheel chairs, no educational tutors, no need to practice with those toes even if he could move them. It was not uncommon for even families to dissociate from such people because they could not care for them. They were too big a burden.

Such conditions have to be understood before we can see this story unfold in front of the religious leaders, the Pharisees and Scribes–those best suited to keeping all the Jewish traditions. They are the ones most concerned with ritual purification and keeping the law in order to be righteous. They have come from all over Judea to hear the new teacher, the one who speaks with such authority. On this particular day, the house where Jesus is staying is filled with the scholars and teachers who have come to see and hear the new hot-shot, the one some are calling Messiah, the one others are now addressing as Rabbi, teacher. They've come to see for themselves, and the place is packed. Luke lets his readers know in advance, however, that more than teaching is in store. The healing power of the Lord is with him. Divine presence is in the room, just as the power of the Holy Spirit accompanied him after his baptism, and just as the Spirit of the Lord was upon him in Nazareth.

Into that setting come five men–four men carrying a pallet bearing a man who is paralyzed. Imagine being in the crowd for a moment. Perhaps you saw some guys outside the window a few moments earlier. But then you began to hear the noise of people taking the outside stairway to the roof. Think about the struggle to carry the man and the pallet up those stairs. Finally the noise of getting up there dies down. Your attention is just beginning to shift back to the teacher when you begin to hear people on the roof and it sounds like they are tearing something up. Now it is not just the noise but dirt and dust falling on your head as somebody starts taking the roof apart, pulling up tiles, creating this unwanted skylight in the midst of the most important lecture you've ever attended. Imagine being the owner of the house that someone is tearing up before your very eyes! Who can pay attention to Jesus now? Then you discover the true source of trouble. These four guys start lowering a pallet that obviously has some invalid on it. Who would have such audacity and rudeness?

Suddenly your attention is back on the teacher–what will he do with this interruption? Who are those impudent men on the roof who would dare to interrupt the teacher? Jesus sees the faith of those four men: men willing to treat a non-person, a paralytic, with such care and concern that they would first carry him to the place where Jesus was. Then, for the sake of this outcast person, they risk the liability claims of tearing up another man's house in order to get this invalid before the one they believe has power to heal.

With the paralyzed man lying in front of him and all the Pharisees and teachers watching, Jesus says, "Man, your sins are forgiven." Aside from the belief often shared by people then that the paralysis was the result of sin–a belief that Jesus would dispel on other occasions, by the way–the truth is that this man had no access even to the Jewish sacrifices as a means of forgiveness, so the statement had great power and the man did have great need. But the immediate question in the audience is, "Who gave him authority or power to make such pronouncements? Who can forgive sins but God alone?"

As readers of Luke's gospel, as people who believe Jesus to be the Son of God as Luke has repeatedly argued and sought to demonstrate, there is a sense in which we want to say to the crowd, "Exactly! Who can forgive sins but God alone?" That is precisely who Luke claims Jesus is, God in the flesh! But Jesus is facing an audience that only sees a human, a teacher perhaps, but now a dangerous one who blasphemes, who makes God-claims for himself when they know he is a mere man. Knowing their questions, hearing the murmuring in the crowd, Jesus addresses them: "Which is easier, to say 'Your sins are forgiven,' or to say, 'Rise up and walk?'" The fact is, then or now, both are impossible, aren't they? With all of our medical technology, nobody can say to Mike, "Rise up and walk!"

Who alone but the creator of the universe can forgive sins? Who can make paralysis suddenly disappear? "But to prove my identity and demonstrate that the Son of Man has authority to forgive sins–rise, take up your pallet and walk out of here!" And the man does, immediately–with no hesitation. What a sight that must have been! If you could see Mike, or if you have seen other victims of paralysis, you know how atrophied the muscle and tissue becomes. Mike's legs are about as big around as a tangerine. I can't imagine how much time and exercise would be required to develop the muscle tissue and ligaments to the point of him being able to walk if the paralysis were suddenly gone. But the claim of this story is, no physical therapy was required, no months of rehab and pain. The man immediately gets up and walks, glorifying God as he leaves the room. "Who can forgive sins but God alone?" "Who is this Son of Man?" This crowd of teachers and Pharisees and all others gathered there join in giving glory to God, filled with awe as they say, "We have seen strange things today." Literally the word used is, "We have seen paradoxes today!" Paradox–that which is beyond opinion, beyond what we understand to be how the world operates–beyond what our heads tell us is true.

The paralytic at the center of these strange events is suddenly fully human again. But even he must ponder those first words of Jesus, "Your sins are forgiven." Forgiveness is one of those words and concepts that seem so obvious on the one hand, so much a part of religious vocabulary, and yet the truth is, it is still a paradox. Oh, we talk about it and pronounce it upon others and thank God for it. We often expect it to function like God's giant Pez dispenser. "Got a problem? Ah, God loves you–pop a forgiveness Pez and forget about it." What you have is not forgiveness or repentance or true confession, but a seared conscience–a paralysis of the soul.

The power of forgiveness lies in understanding the true nature of sin. We live in a world that is constantly redefining and minimizing sin.   Our nation has just endured such redefinition at the highest levels of government. When is a lie really a lie? When is adultery–sex with someone other than one's mate–really adultery? Even at the level of your life and mine, we know how to redefine the truth. We know about spin doctoring–it's what we do with our parents and our teachers. We don't really lie, we just tell the parts of the truth that are most advantageous to us, right? Sin is not really sin anymore. A bit later in Luke's gospel, Jesus will say that there is absolutely nothing hidden that will not be revealed. But in that hidden condition, our spirits become paralyzed. We become numb to the hurt we are inflicting on ourselves and others. I know we are accustomed to definitions of sin that talk about failure to keep the commands of God. But I'm finding a different definition helpful. Sin is that which dehumanizes people–either others or ourselves. To be human is to be more than animals, but less than God. Sin occurs when we act as mere animals, or we treat others as mere animals. Or when we see ourselves as gods–towering over the rest of humanity, better than other people, in no need for God. Alcohol and drugs dehumanize–dull our senses, impair our judgment. Pornography demeans sexuality and the human body, treating it as nothing more than animalistic, without a soul or God-presence. Eating disorders are, in many cases, a result of the deification of our bodies–thinking that a particular shape or look is of absolute importance to our identity. That which degrades another person, that which makes any of us less than a being created in the very image of God, that is sin. That is why Paul can say the whole law is summed up in just one phrase–love your neighbor as yourself.

When Jesus heals this man, he restores his humanity, not once but twice. And the first restoration is more powerful than the second. While this man's paralysis is not evidence of someone's sin, sin in our lives does lead to paralysis. Oh, we may be able to walk and talk and look normal, but our inner selves are seized with fear and anger and guilt and shame. We will go to extravagant lengths to redefine sin so that it is no longer sin, just the struggles of life or no big deal. After all, we're all forgiven anyway. So we minimize sin and minimize forgiveness, keeping it all inside, while we wear nice, smiley faces and go to Christian schools. Deep inside somewhere we know the lie, the falsehood of our existence.

Jesus came to rescue human beings from our inhumane behaviors and circumstances. This paralyzed man was freed from paralysis, not once but twice. What about the paralysis that cripples you in your life?

THE GOOD SAMARITAN

The 'example story' parables in Luke's gospel have long proven a point in our pulpits that we tried to deny in our more academic study of the parables, namely, that there is more than one point to be made in a parable! In preaching we often take great liberty with the parables, asking our audiences to identity with the various characters in the story. We also find ourselves quickly drawn to allegory when we preach the parables, while saying all along that allegory is not appropriate to exegesis of the parables. I am not sure on which side I err in attempting to create a hearing for this text among college students at Lipscomb University. My goal was to take the message away from the stranded motorist on the Interstate and bring the neighbor back into the neighborhood.

THE GOOD SAMARITAN
LUKE 10:25-37

One of the casualties of modern television viewing is the Wild West of American history. When I was growing up it seemed like there was some kind of cowboy show on every night. From the Lone Ranger to Bonanza to Wagon Train to the Virginian to Rawhide to Gunsmoke, you could always find a cowboy show to watch. And if you went to the movies, there was usually a John Wayne, or a Kirk Douglas, or later, a Clint Eastwood cowboy movie. Everyone knew the law of the west was the six-gun at the hero's hip. One never knew when the gunfight would erupt, but there always would be at least one in every show. As they told the tale week after week, there was no room for the faint hearted in the West; Indians or robbers or scoundrels were as prevalent as aliens in the X Files. It was a fearful time to live; only the brave survived. In our time of course, there is law and order, the streets are all safe, and we live without fear and without carrying guns, right? No, that's not quite right anymore. One is not safe from theft, even on this campus. Then there are those other parts of Nashville–the parts where some of you work; the parts where guns show up at school sometimes, the parts that you would not dare drive alone at night.

Use the image of the Old West with me this morning, or perhaps the image of the urban jungle like L.A. and you're out for a Sunday drive on the freeways. Imagine traveling alone through a section of town or perhaps the country that is notorious for thieves and gang warfare. A section of the road where even soldiers have been attacked, but you are traveling alone. It's fairly rugged terrain, reminds you a lot of those old movies you saw in which there is some cut-throat behind every tree and around every corner. Imagine making that trip and having your worst fears come true. You round the bend of the road and you're attacked from all sides. Before you really know what has happened, you're being beaten senseless, your clothes are being torn off, you're battered and bleeding and finally unconscious. More than being mugged, you've nearly been killed. It's an isolated stretch of road that only fools like yourself travel alone, and you have no idea if or when any kind of help may arrive. You just lie there, baking in the sun, unable to holler for help, helpless to bind your own wounds, going from conscious to semi-conscious.

After what seems to be hours, you hear the sound of another person coming. You want to yell or wave for help but you can't. The person comes near, sees you–you know he sees you—but he stops and stares and looks around and then with great fear hurries on by leaving you to rot in the sun. And you wait some more. Who knows if anyone ever will come by and help. Finally, hours later, someone again is on that deserted road. Once more, they at least stop, but they too just stare for awhile; then their eyes begin to dart all around, as though expecting the thieves to return at any moment, and they hasten on off.

And in your broken, bleeding, delirious condition, you are left to wait. Finally you lose consciousness. It is days later, in a bed, in a hospital that you regain consciousness. When you are aware enough to ask, you want to know what happened. How did you get here? And someone tells you the story–an Iraqi who spoke no English brought you in. An AIDS patient found you beside the road and bound your wounds. Whoever it is that you have always been trained to hate was the one who had the courage to stop and bind your wounds and bring you in. More than that, your hospital bill was paid in advance by this stranger.

It is hard to tell the parable of the Good Samaritan today, because we've already heard it too many times, and my re-telling this morning falls short in many ways of capturing the moment in Jesus'life when a wise and understanding teacher of the law tried to trick Jesus. I've left out all the details in the discussion that prompted the story: a lawyer's rhetorical question about inheriting eternal life. Jesus had just finished telling his disciples how thankful he was that the kingdom had not been revealed to the wise and understanding but to infants and babes when this man started up. He already was quite sure of himself and his own answers when he asked the question. But Jesus knew that also when he turned the question back on him and said, "How do you read?" With some pride, no doubt, the lawyer responded by quoting the great commandments: "Love the Lord your God with all your heart, soul, strength, and mind. Love your neighbor as yourself." And Jesus would have been pleased to leave it there, but the lawyer still needed to show off, still needed to justify himself by getting Jesus to define the boundaries of the neighborhood. Who is it that I need to love as myself?

The answer given, of course, was not what he wanted to hear. Your neighbor is the person who has the courage to stop in very dangerous circumstances and drag you to safety when you're about to die. Likewise, you are called to act as neighbor toward others you might see in such need of help. What a shock to the lawyer's system it must have been to admit that his religious peers did not love their neighbors as themselves. Both the priest and the Levite at first appeared as givers of life and hope, but then they just ignored the needs and walked on by. I used to think that the main reason these two passed by was their legal code. If they touched a dead man they would be ceremonially unclean. But I have come to believe that, more than thinking about keeping the Law, they did not see a real person there—just an object. No matter what the motives of the priest or Levite, the greater problem for the lawyer was not who didn't stop, but who did! Jesus says it was a low-life Samaritan who actually came to the rescue.

One question that this parable forces each one of us to ask is, who is worthy of our help? Who is it in our lives that we would consider unworthy as the lawyer considered the Samaritan unworthy? That is not just a question about those we would refuse to help, but those we would not want to help us! Who is worth being rescued by us, and how far are we willing to go in risking ourselves on their behalf? How much of our own fears are we willing to face in order to help others who are hurting? This is not just about stopping on I-40 to help a stranded motorist, although that's part of it. It's not just about riding the inner city bus through the projects tomorrow night, although again, that's certainly part of it. It is also about our ability to care for, and nurse back to health, even the people right here in our midst who are hurting and we keep passing by on the other side of the road. We just don't see those who are struggling with eating disorders that are about to destroy them. We never see the guys addicted to pornography whose double lives are literally eating them alive. We don't see the people that are loners–oh, we see them but we never quite have a conversation with them. We don't see international students who struggle with English, we avoid what we cannot understand– and vice versa. We see people who have sat on the same row with us throughout this semester but; we have no clue what their names are.

Yes, there is still the neighborhood out there, filled with those people and places and parts of Nashville that we wish would go away or we wish the cops could control better. Yes, it is a good thing when we have the courage to help a stranded motorist, especially in these fearful times when thieves do use that ploy just as they did in the first century to gain another victim. But some of us here this morning are also beaten and bleeding inside. God forbid that we have to wait until the person we most love to hate offers us assistance!

The people in need of mercy are right here this morning. Someone suggested to me as I was struggling with this lesson that I just needed to go watch Mr. Roger's Neighborhood. You all remember that show from your childhood. Fred begins every show with a line that I want to close with this morning. Fred invites every viewer into his audience by asking "Would you be my neighbor?" I ask you this morning, "Would you be my neighbor?" Would you be neighbor to the stranger sitting five seats over from you? Would you be neighbor to the person in front you that you've been trying to see around every day for the past semester? Do you need Jesus to have mercy on you this morning?

WHEN SERVICE BECOMES SERVITUDE

Tom Long's discussion of the pronouncement stories has prompted me to think through this particular text with an eye on Martha's audacity in trying to correct not just her sister, but Jesus! In this sermon, I attempt to get the audience to understand the social boundaries that are violated in the story because of the higher calling and social identity offered to one who finds identity in Jesus Messiah. Too often, our religious activity becomes the same roadblock to relationship with God in Christ. We are doing the right things, but no longer with the right heart. Worse yet, we begin to wonder why God doesn't take sides and fix the inequities of our efforts.

WHEN SERVICE BECOME SERVITUDE
LUKE 10:38-42

When I was preaching for the Western Hills church in Temple, Texas in the early 1990s, the congregation had its 85th anniversary as a church. The congregation had been in the same location for last 25 of those years, and there were people who still remembered the early years and the previous locations of the building. The preacher before me, James LeFan, was minister for almost half of those years. He preached for 39 years and became an elder of the church in his "semi-retirement." I loved to listen to James and others reflect on the changes that had occurred in church life over those decades. There were marvelous stories about the growth of the congregation, the birthing of two other congregations in town, the great gospel meetings, the saints who had served faithfully year after year. While I was there, Mollie Spoonts retired from teaching the third grade. She had been the Sunday morning third grade teacher for 37 years. Thirty-seven years without a break teaching a Sunday School class! You may know of people in this congregation that have been at it that long or longer. But such continuous years of service are rare anymore. Life is too full; there are too many working moms, too many other activities that vie for our time and attention. Most Sunday School coordinators are hoping to get one–or two–quarter commitments, not two–or–three decade commitments. The same is often true for most other areas of service in the church. Just finding people to fill and clean communion trays month to month is difficult. That is true in spite of all our technological advances and time management solutions and apparent flexibility of schedules. We all seem to live in a world in which time is such a precious commodity and we have too much to accomplish and too little time to get it done.

With such tremendous competition for our time, we now talk about workaholics and burn–out–people whose stress levels and work loads finally reach a breaking point. They need to reduce their load and activity, either at church or at work or both. I don't know that it was any easier to find teachers or commit-tee leaders in 1965 than it is today. I do know that in any age, the call to service can create feelings and attitudes that lead to problems–not just burn-out, but animosity and bitterness. Those who serve become exasperated by those who do not. Many of us are familiar with the old 80-20 rule: 80% of the work of the church is done by 20% of the people. George Barna claims, by the way, that as we begin the 21st century, the 80-20 rule has become the 95-5 rule. Now 5% are doing 95% of the work of the church. And how many of the 5% aren't surviving in service and ministry? They keep serving when they would love to have a break because no one else will step in and help out. They begin to resent the fact that they have to work while others merely watch. They resent the fact that their Sundays are filled with three or four meeting times while others have trouble committing to one; their Saturdays or Monday nights are always committed because others won't commit to one a month or once every two weeks. They begin to focus not on the service they are rendering and the knowledge they themselves are gaining, but on their burden of overwork. The resentment can be even stronger among the server's family. The spouse resents the husband or wife always being gone, especially if it is for extra things at church! The meeting times and the committees and the activities themselves turn into curses instead of blessings, not just for those who don't show up and perhaps feel pains of guilt, but for those who do show up, for whom church activities become a competition for their time instead of a blessing from God. When church becomes a chore and one more activity to squeeze in instead of an oasis, then something has gone wrong.

The story read earlier from Luke 10 reminds us that the tension over serving has been around a long time. But here more is at stake than showing up for a meeting. Remember the context of Luke chapter 10. Jesus has just told the parable of the good Samaritan to a lawyer who came asking Jesus what he needed to do to inherit eternal life. The lawyer was not satisfied with keeping the two great commandments–love God with all your heart, soul, mind, and strength; love your neighbor as yourself. He wanted to specify his responsibility by getting Jesus to define the term "neighbor." In telling the parable, Jesus forced the Jewish lawyer to identify with the neighborliness of a hated Samaritan, in contrast to the priest and the Levite–two respected Jewish religious leaders. The lawyer had to give up his biased attitudes about Samaritans by being called to act like a Samaritan instead of like the Jewish leaders.

Now, Jesus comes to a village where he goes against all the

rules of decency according to those same Jewish leaders. A Jewish teacher would never enter the house of a woman–the Pharisees would not even speak to women on the street. Jesus enters the house of two women–and her sister Mary. Martha immediately busies herself doing what women do and did in that culture–the honorable thing for a woman to do was to serve the male guest. The sister Mary, on the other hand, does something outrageous and unheard of–she sits at the feet of Jesus. The phrase "To sit at the feet" denotes becoming a disciple, a student of a great teacher. The apostle Paul is described as having sat at the feet of Gamaliel, a great Jewish teacher. Women were never allowed to be students of the rabbi. Even in Greek and Roman culture, women never could teach others because they were not allowed to be taught themselves. Jesus does the unthinkable, first by entering a woman's house, and then accepting a woman as a disciple.

Martha, on the other hand, is hard at it, doing what women do. And it dawns on her that she is being cheated. She's doing all the work while her sister sits around, breaking all the social boundaries of acceptable behavior. Martha is doing the honorable thing in serving; Mary is acting as a student with (her!) teacher. That which is honorable becomes enslaving and bitter. Martha finally appeals to the teacher to make her sister get off the ground and do some work. In so doing, Martha also violates the boundaries of social behavior by asking a stranger to intervene. But more than changing Mary's behavior, she is trying to correct Jesus' behavior in giving private instruction to a woman. But Jesus rebukes Martha–rebukes her, the one doing all of the work! "Martha, Martha, you are anxious and troubled about many things" (your priorities are all messed up!). "One thing is needful–Mary has chosen the good portion."

"Man does not live by bread alone but by every word that proceeds from the mouth of God." Rather than acting according to the social customs and demands of her time, Mary had chosen to sit at the feet of the teacher–a socially unacceptable thing for a woman to do. Martha's busyness had cost her an opportunity to learn, to spend time with the Word of God that came in the flesh.

It is possible for Christian service to become embittered slavery. It is possible for a good servant to lose the focus of love and the spirit of Jesus in serving and instead be just like

Martha–missing the presence of God because of one's Christian duty. It is possible for teenagers to feel they're forced to be here, and to never experience the presence of God or find any meaning in being here. No matter what the length of your own Christian walk, it is possible to lose sight of why any of this is important. It becomes a job, a duty to be performed. I heard the story this week of a minister who who retired after preaching for over 45 years. The day he retired he stopped going to church–been there, done that for too long.

So what is Luke trying to say to us through this story? Perhaps it is this: Loving God with all one's heart, mind, soul and strength means that one first has to spend time with Jesus before service can be rendered and sustained. It takes time to become holy, to grow into the identity we have received as a trust in Christ. Those who fail to take time away from the busyness of life, those who fail to take time to be in the presence of Messiah, to take seriously the promise of presence, to listen to the Word of God in scripture and in prayer–such people do not have much of a relationship with God in the end. People who get so busy serving in the church that they fail to sit at the feet of Jesus. Those are the people who suffer burn-out and disappear. Multiplying activities at the church building is helpful only if those activities contribute to holiness. Your being here today is helpful only if it contributes to holiness, to your becoming more like Jesus. If you come to church thinking you are doing God a favor, if this is your contribution to God, you've got it all backwards.

But there is another problem that many of us who see ourselves as the real workers in the church share with Martha. We object to all of those others we see around us who don't hop up and help us out! We suffer from the comparison game! On the one hand, we need to do the right thing, so that has us scurrying around in activity. But it's not long before we begin to tire, and we then notice that so many others aren't scurrying with us. In fact, we're carrying their load as well as our own! Never mind that, like Mary, the activity of others may be less visible but no less needful. Never mind that we are wearied in our well-doing to the point of turning our frustration on others and accusing them of laziness or false motives or even false spirituality. At that moment, our own spirituality in service has proved false.

Do not misunderstand me this morning. To become like Jesus is to lay down one's life in service to others. To become like Jesus is to seek and save the lost. But only those who sit at the feet of Jesus and take time to become like him have the power and spiritual strength to sustain their service to others. Christian maturity is just like physical maturity. We begin as infants and grow into adolescence and hopefully into spiritual adulthood. If we assign the jobs of the church to the infants, what will happen? If we fail to train the infants and feed them and help them grow, what happens? If we fail to train them to be responsible in those pre-teen and adolescent years, what will happen?

I suggest to you that Christian burn-out usually has to do with the failure to take time to be holy, the failure to spend time at the feet of Jesus. Yes, service and deed are important. But if the activity precedes the listening, if prayer and Word get sacrificed in the time crunch, even the most dedicated servant will grow cold and lose sight of the one thing that is needful. As we look toward a new decade and a new millenium, it is hard to imagine more exciting opportunities, a more vibrant life together than what God is giving to us now. It is also easy to envision the current pace eating people alive, with service turning to servitude, and today's joys and successes becoming next year's flame-outs and cynics. Only time at the feet of Jesus will see us through. Is there that time built into your life for 2000? Or is it time, today, to make a change?

Have you given your soul, your life, your all to Jesus? In Christ Jesus, God offers to make us saints! Holy ones. Such identity can only be the gift of God. Living that identity can be reality only if we nurture the vision of who we are. Is this church business all a chore that upsets you because others aren't pulling their weight? One thing is needful. Choose the good portion.

FINDING FAITH ON EARTH

In chapter four of this volume, Greg Sterling locates one of Luke's purposes for emphasizing prayer in serving as an "antidote to apostasy as the disciples face the long view of history." The "already, not yet" view of history that Luke takes necessitates the need for persistence in prayer. The parables on prayer that begin chapter eighteen in Luke's gospel are conditioned by all that has preceded them. In the case of the widow and the unjust judge, this story is intended by Luke to be seen not only through the lens of the initial commentary pray and do not lose heart) but also through the larger interests in the gospel of God's faithful response to the disenfranchised. In this sermon, I want to be faithful to the larger context, particularly in chapter seventeen, of the "already, not yet" experience of the kingdom in Luke, and Luke's portrayal of prayer while we await the "not yet." As we enter a third millennium since the "fullness of time" act of God in Christ, believing in the "already, not yet" of kingdom presence is at the heart of faithful prayer. The question of Jesus with regard to the commonness of prayer and our faith claims is crucial to faithful living.

FINDING FAITH ON EARTH
LUKE 18:1-8

In his book *Prayer: Finding the Heart's True Home*, Richard Foster says

> coming to prayer is like coming home. Nothing feels more right, more like what we are created to be and to do. Yet at the same time we are confronted with great mysteries. Who hasn't struggled with the puzzle of unanswered prayer? Who hasn't wondered how a finite person can commune with the infinite Creator of the Universe? Who hasn't questioned whether prayer isn't merely psychological manipulation after all? We do our best, of course, to answer these knotty questions but when all is said and done, there is a sense in which these mysteries remain unanswered and unanswerable...At such times we must learn to become comfortable with the mystery. [1]

In the opening chapter of the book Foster addresses the human agendas that often drive our prayers.

> The truth of the matter is, we all come to prayer with a tangled mass of motives–altruistic and selfish, merciful and hateful, loving and bitter. Frankly, this side of eternity we will never unravel the good from the bad, the pure from the impure. But what I have come to see is that God is big enough to receive us with all our mixture. We do not have to be bright, or pure, or filled with faith, or anything. That is what grace means, and not only are we saved by grace, we lived by it as well. And we pray by it.

I appreciate Foster's candor and insight about a subject that we all know and yet none of us know. There are unanswerable mysteries about prayer, about this conversation that always seems one-sided–at least when we, re-engaged in it. On the one hand, we say that God knows our thoughts before we can

---

[1] Richard Foster, *Prayer: Finding the Heart's True Home* (Harper: San Francisco, 1992).

verbalize them, that the Holy Spirit intercedes when we have no words. On the other hand, without that verbalization process we often fall prey to no conversation with God at all. There is the mystery of prayers answered and seemingly unanswered. There are the stock phrases and routine prayer that can become mindless and, for us humans at least, meaningless. There is this thing we do here on Sundays called "public prayer" which we then distinguish from "private prayer." With public prayer there is always the question of audience. Very often the prayers found in scripture clearly are intended as much for a human audience as they are intended for God.

This parable and the next one in Luke have to do with prayer. The context for the two parables on prayer that open chapter 18 is the discussion in the previous chapter regarding the kingdom of God. If you look back at chapter 17, that discussion begins with a question from Pharisees, the religious leaders who seemed always to be questioning and doubting the authenticity of Jesus and his message. When they ask Jesus when the Kingdom of God is coming, he tells them that is the wrong question. There are no signs to be observed that would predict the reign of God, nor people crying "here it is, or there it is," because the kingdom, the reign of God, is in their midst. The presence of Messiah among them has already ushered in the reign of God. They are rejecting Jesus and therefore rejecting the reign of God in their midst. Jesus then immediately turns to his disciples to remind them that his presence is temporary and the reign of God not yet totally complete. The time is coming when they will long for one of the days of the Son of Man, and not see it. Again, the issue is not about watching for signs of the times. When he does appear it will be as obvious to all as lightning that flashes across the whole sky. But first he must suffer and be rejected by that generation.

Luke's audiences would have heard these words two generations later, when Jesus was long since crucified, resurrected and ascended into heaven. They were among those waiting and longing to see a day of the Son of Man. Jesus' warnings to not be like the people in the days of Noah or the people of Sodom would have been just as appropriate to them as to us. The potential for losing heart, for deciding he really wasn't coming soon, for becoming consumed with the daily affairs of life on earth was great. Thus, the warning to not be like

Lot's wife and be too tied to this world and its cares and pleasures.

Our chapter division at that point disguises the fact that Jesus continues in that same context to tell two parables about prayer, first addressing the disciples and then addressing the Pharisees. He uses a common Jewish argument in which, if a lesser condition is true, the greater is much more so. The example he chooses highlights the plight of a widow, one of three kinds of people especially protected in Jewish law, along with sojourners and orphans. Because the widow had no social standing in community unless she also had children to care for her, she could be subject at times to great injustice. Deuteronomy 27:19 pronounces a curse upon anyone who deprives the sojourner, the orphan or the widow of justice. Yet, here is a widow, Jesus says, who has been unjustly treated. Worse yet, she pleads her case before a judge who couldn't care less about God or his laws, or people in general. Perhaps he is a Gentile, perhaps a Jew who is one ethnically but not religiously. The widow pleads and he refuses to help. But finally he vindicates her simply because he's tired of her bothering him. The original language suggests he is afraid of the notoriety that may embarrass him by her continued presence, his continued rejection of her pleas. Jesus says, "hear what the unrighteous judge says. Will not God vindicate his elect who cry out to him day and night? Will he delay long over them. I tell you he will vindicate them speedily (could also be "suddenly")." If a no-count judge can be moved by this widow's persistent pleading to act in her behalf, how much more will God do for those who continually cry out to him?

Nevertheless, Jesus says, when the Son of Man comes will he find faith on earth? The question takes us right back into the previous discussion of people distracted by the cares and pleasures of the world to the point that they miss the reign of God and the return of the Son of Man when he comes. Will people have faith? Will they always pray and not lose heart? One translation reads, "he told them this parable with the point that it is necessary to continue praying without giving up."

For those of us waiting for the Son of Man to appear almost 2000 years later, Jesus' question is only more appropriate. We ought to be longing for the day of the Son of Man, but after this long period of time, most of us–even in this Y2K season–become distracted by the routines of human existence on earth to the point that we no longer really believe it will happen. Few of us live in great expectation for his coming. Who of us prays continually for his return? Who of us prays continually for the vindication of his people against the temptations and evils of this world? How many times should you pray before you've prayed enough–about anything. Sometimes we think that once God knows, we can stop talking–but God knew before we opened our minds or our mouths. That's not the point, is it? Prayer is the communicative process that keeps us connected to God. It is his communicative gift to us, for our benefit. When people stop talking, it is a sure sign they have given up on a relationship, isn't it? That's true in marriage, in every social relationship and circumstance. No communication equals no relationship. In the immediate context of this parable, clearly the content of prayer has to do with praying for and expecting the return of the Son of man, continually praying and not giving up just because God's timing does not seem to correspond with ours.

But the principle of prayer and its power in our lives is much bigger than that. Faithful people will be found when the Son of man does come only if people are in relationship, only if they have continued the conversation and the life focus that comes from that conversation. In the closest of relationships there is nothing off limits in conversation. Nothing hidden, nothing that cannot be talked about. So it is with prayer. It is not a time in life, it is a way of life. It is more than a debate over public and private prayer, bigger than the clichés that entrap our language of prayer, it is believing in a relationship with Creator God that calls us into constant conversation and awareness of that relationship and trust in that relationship. It is faith and faithfulness.

There is also no moment with God when we have said it enough and don't need to speak any more. The continual praying has to do with our focus and awareness, not with God's. In the prayer life of this body of believers, when do we decide that we have prayed about something or someone enough? And if prayer for the present and future of our individual lives is continuous, then what about our prayer for this congregation as a body of believers called by God to ministry in this place at this time. It is easy to pray about the Togo mission with Don and

Jane in our midst—but will the prayer continue when they are in Africa? What is God up to at the Donelson church? For those of us not in attendance on Tuesday nights, what do we think is happening in those weekly prayer sessions? How constant is our conversation about our present and our future, our strengths and our weaknesses? How often do we lift up this body and give God the praise and glory for who we are, what we have become, and what God envisions for our future? What do we pray for when we ask God to bless this congregation?

The conversation with God must go on. Those who have been in constant conversation must be joined by the rest of us who are slow to catch on and carry on. What marvelous things God is doing because of the faith of those who have been persistent in prayer throughout the history of this body in this location. My question this evening is, who will join us? Who will pursue the life of faith that is so continuous in prayer? Who will renew their focus of God and their commitment to him in prayer and their witness to the world that Jesus is Lord your souls?

HUMBLE YOURSELVES BEFORE THE LORD

For anyone reading through Luke's gospel to this point, the "rest of the story" is apparent in the introduction of Jesus' parable. Luke consistently characterizes the Pharisees as those who "trust in themselves that they were righteous and despised others" (18:9). Likewise the tax collectors and sinners are always portrayed as those most receptive to the redemptive activity of Jesus. At every turn in this parable, therefore, it is difficult to find the "surprise" of the parable, the twist in the story that "teases the mind into active awareness." However, in Luke's time as well as ours, I imagine, identifying too quickly with the humble leads to our being more accurately identified with the self-exaltation of the Pharisee. It is a frightening thought to face the vulnerability of right hearts being "justified" and right performance going away empty.

In his commentary on this passage, Luke Johnson writes, "Prayer is faith in action. It is not an optional exercise in piety, carried out to demonstrate one's relationship with God. It is that relationship with God. The way one prays therefore reveals that relationship." And then he adds, "If prayer is self-assertion before God, then it cannot be answered by God's gift of righteousness; possession and gift cancel each other."[2] Remember that this parable and the one preceding in verses 1-8 are a continuation of Jesus telling the Pharisees and the disciples how to live in the absence of the Son of Man. This conversation started when Pharisees asked about the coming of the kingdom of God. Jesus replied that the reign of God was already in their midst, but then he told the disciples that completion of the reign of God among humans would come only after the Son of Man returned. First he must suffer and be rejected by this generation. He would be taken from then, but then he would return again. The question was, would people be faithful in his absence? Would they be ready for his return? Would they be like the people in the days of Noah or Lot who became so interested in the realities of life on earth that they were all destroyed by their lack of faith and watchfulness? The first parable on prayer that Luke presents in this context is the story of the widow crying out to a judge who did not care about God or humans, but because she kept bothering him, the judge finally gave her justice. How much more, Jesus says, will your heavenly Father respond to your requests. Nevertheless, Jesus asks, when the son of man comes, will he find faith on earth? It is the people who stay in constant conversation with God, who keep themselves from falling into the trap of the people in Noah's day or in the days of Sodom. Prayer is that incredible gift from God that keeps humans focused on kingdom life and kingdom business rather than on the cares and activities of this life only.

In this second parable on prayer, Jesus goes on to address the posture of prayer: not the physical posture, but the spiritual

---

[2] Luke Timothy Johnson, *The Gospel of Luke*, Sacra Pagina Series (Collegeville, MN: Liturgical Press, 1991), 274.

and mental posture. What self-understanding do I bring before God in prayer? As he did with the previous parable, Luke tells us what the content of the parable is about before we read it. "Jesus also told this parable to some who trusted in themselves that they were righteous and despised others." If you read through the previous 17 chapters of Luke's account, there can be no doubt who these people are. It is the people who complain that Jesus eats with tax collectors and sinners, the people who are always watching Jesus that they might trap him in some unlawful deed or saying. It is the religious, particularly the Pharisees, who have such self-confidence, and their view of themselves has created an exclusiveness towards others. The story Jesus tells immediately proves our expectations correct. Two men went up to pray, one a Pharisee and one a tax collector. The Pharisee does what righteous people do–he stands boldly and looks into heaven and gives thanks for all the goodness in his life. But there are two problems with his prayer. The first is that his self-understanding as a righteous person creates an attitude of superiority towards other people. "I sure am glad I'm better than those kinds of people–extortioners, unjust, adulterers, even that guy over there, the tax collector." Luke even says that such people despise others–they become bigoted in their outlook of other people. The second problem is, he gives himself credit for that goodness. "I fast twice a week, I give tithes of all that I get." Here is a guy who not only keeps all of the religious rules, he goes beyond the rules. Remember the scandal of this story, even in the midst of our expectations. Tithing is good, isn't it? There is no blessing in being a thief, or adulterer, or tax collecting. The question is, who shall receive credit for that goodness? Even his prayer time is a reflection of his piety as he asserts his own goodness before God.

In contrast there is the all–but–pagan tax collector, the one who has sold out his Jewish identity by working for the foreign government, making a living by charging more than the government requires. He had to sneak into the temple because everyone knows he doesn't belong there. Being too ashamed to look up, standing far–off, he beats his breast and cries out, "Be merciful to me, a sinner." There are no righteous deeds by which he can assert himself and his own goodness before God. He can only plead for God to be merciful to him. And Jesus says that it is the tax collector's prayer that was heard on that occasion, not the Pharisee's. And he repeats the proverb that Jesus first uttered back in chapter 14: *Everyone who exalts himself will be humbled; everyone who humbles himself will be exalted.*

Prayer is faith in action. It is not an optional exercise in piety, carried on to demonstrate one's relationship with God. I sure am thankful none of us is like that Pharisee, aren't you? The ironic twist of this parable comes when we try to figure out which character we most identify with. You see, on the one hand, none of us want to be the Pharisee. Yet, he is the one in the story whose life would fit the best in this auditorium this morning. A man with religious convictions. A man who understands he has been blessed by God. A man who makes sure he keeps his life focused by fasting and tithing and praying. The problem is that those attributes are not gifts from God but possessions and self-accomplishments that he lists before God. They are the jewels in his crown that he proudly displays before God. And with his accomplishments there is also an attitude toward other people. Those who have less and do less than him are worth less in his opinion. People who don't perform like he performs become the "less-thans," the people to be scorned or despised, Luke says.

On the other hand, the life of the tax collector is no model existence to be followed, except in his self-understanding before God. What makes the tax collector the good guy in this story is his humbling himself before the Lord. Nothing else about him is commendable. But he does understand prayer. He does understand that righteousness is a gift to be received, not a merit badge to be possessed and announced. If we say, "I sure am glad I'm like the tax collector and not like the Pharisee," what have we done? All such comparisons of ourselves to other people are made for the same reasons. But before God, in prayer, we bring only ourselves, without any comparisons or rationales or excuses.

Such statements are made to justify ourselves, either for ourselves or for other people. Think of how different life would be without those comparisons, not just in our prayer life but in how we live and think at all times. How many times do we justify ourselves by pointing out how much better we are than other people? Is God not listening when we do that? People come to their boss and ask for a raise and the reason that they give is, "Well Jack gets more than I do, and I work harder than

Jack." Or the comparisons we make on campus with other students, to whom we feel superior…. Trusting in one's own accomplishments necessitates distinguishing those accomplishments from others. We are always better than or worse than in such comparisons.

Prayer is faith in action. When we come before God, we have nothing that can be hidden, but we also have nothing to merit his attention or his blessing or his offer of relationship. It is not with whom we are in relationship that matters at that moment, it is who we understand ourselves to be before God. He who exalts himself will be humbled; he who humbles himself will be exalted.

What is true of those times when we stop to verbally pray is true the rest of the time as well. None of life is lived outside the presence and knowledge of God. All of life is lived in the context of relationship with God if we have been given relationship by his grace through Jesus Christ. There is a sense, therefore, in which all of life is lived in prayer, in conversation with God; whether we are addressing him directly or not–he certainly is aware of our conversation.

So, whom do we trust when we are not in a church building or someplace like this that we associate with being spiritual–or at least being religious? Whose accomplishments merit attention when we are away from church? And what kinds of people are beneath us in other settings? Does God not hear us when we use racial slurs, or tell racist jokes? When we offer bigoted assessments of others, does that not count because we did not say, "Dear God" first? If our attitudes towards others and our lives lived portray our confidence in ourselves and our own accomplishments, and our scorn for other people, what is prayer at that point except an optional exercise in piety, carried out to demonstrate our claimed relationship with God?

And what about the religious snobbery that sometimes says, "I thank God that I am in the right church building with the right sign out front, and the right doctrine inside and not like those other people…" God, be merciful to me a sinner, this morning–and every morning. The more honest I am with myself, the less self-righteousness I have to bring before God.

Prayer is faith in action. It is relationship with God. The way one prays, therefore, reveals that relationship. If prayer is self-assertion before God, then it cannot be answered by God's gift of righteousness; possession and gift cancel each other out. Is righteousness a gift or a possession in your life this morning? If it is a gift, then you have come before the Lord as the tax collector. If it is a possession, a right that you have earned, then you have come thanking God you are not like other people.

Perhaps we all need to humble ourselves before the Lord and pray for his tender mercies to transform our attitudes and actions that we might no longer trust in ourselves and despise others, but live our lives in prayerful faith.

GOD OF THE IMPOSSIBLE

In my experience of preaching through Luke, nothing was more difficult than Luke's repetitious message about rich and poor in the kingdom. As Tim Kelly so strongly points out, we live in a cultural context in which we white, middle class, Christians have great difficulty being honest with this message. While I realize that this particular sermon on the rich ruler may be used to justify—or at least avoid confronting—our materialism, it is intended to help us all face our affluence and the message of Luke with honesty and integrity. The reader can decide whether the sermon is successful in that attempt.

GOD OF THE IMPOSSIBLE
LUKE 18:15-30

This week, I received a phone call from a student at Lipscomb inquiring about a class that I am scheduled to teach in the spring. He wanted to know about the reading requirements for the course, so I told him about the texts that I was going to use. Then he asked about other books that he might read that would be helpful, and I suggested one that was a bit more introductory, thinking he might be trying to become familiar with some basics before the class started. When he heard the title, he said, "Oh, I read that back in undergraduate class." It was one of those "been there, done that" responses. It turned out he wasn't planning on taking the class, he just had an interest in the texts I required. Most of the time when a student asks that kind of question, the real question is, "what must I do to pass this course?" When I was a student, I always wanted to know what the requirements were. That's the part of the syllabus you read first. Who cares about the objectives of learning! The issue is, what must I do? My experience with students over the years has been that very few enter a class asking, "how much can I learn?" Certainly they are there to learn, but the minimum daily requirements for that process are foremost on the student's mind.

In the world of jobs and schedules and employment, many people maintain the same approach. What must I do to keep my job? What must I do to receive a promotion? It ends up remaining that minimum requirement approach to life. The really successful people may say, "what must I do to succeed, to achieve all of my goals?" That extra push may make them work harder, but the question still remains, "what must I do to get whatever it is I want?"

Our story from Luke today takes that question one step farther, as the ruler comes and asks Jesus about the requirements for entering eternal life. His question is the same as that asked by the lawyer back in chapter ten. There the lawyer asked the question to test Jesus. Here the circumstances appear to be different. There is nothing in the context to suggest any devious motive on the part of the man who asks the question. The literary context in which we find the story, however, is very interesting. Remember that the parable that precedes this story in chapter eighteen ends with the proverbial reminder, "Everyone who exalts himself will be humbled, everyone who humbles himself will be exalted." The parable of the Pharisee and tax collector ends a rather extended scene in which Jesus has been talking about the kingdom of God as both a present and future reality. "The reign of God is in your midst," he tells the Pharisees. Yet, there will also be a time when the disciples will long to see a day of the Son of Man and they will not see him. The warnings about readiness for his return at the end of chapter seventeen and the two parables on prayer are all intended to keep followers of Jesus focused on God, relying on prayer and God's sustenance while we await the return of the Son of Man. Those relying on themselves, or those who become too comfortable with life on earth, buying and selling, eating and drinking, building and planting–even those relying on their own pious deeds–may miss the final fruition of Kingdom life with God.

Following the proverb, Luke tells of two more incidents that really illustrate the same principles. First there is the story of families bringing their babies to be touched and blessed by Jesus. When the disciples discover that Jesus' time is being taken up with such trivial pursuits, they chastise the parents for wasting Jesus'time. After all, babies are not really even human yet. They had no legal standing until their teenage years. You don't waste the teacher's time with babies. But Jesus immediately reverses the disciples, telling the parents to come on, and the disciples to get out of the way. "Allow the little children to come to me. Don't hinder them, for the kingdom of God is made of up of such as these. Indeed, whoever does not receive the kingdom as a little child, will never enter into it." Does that mean we receive the kingdom like we receive babies? Or, perhaps more likely, we are to be like babies in order to enter the kingdom? What is it about these babies that makes them kingdom recipients?

Without further commentary by Jesus or Luke, the story continues with the question of the ruler, "Good Teacher, what shall I do to inherit eternal life?" His question still fits the larger context of the nature of the Kingdom and kingdom people. The reign of God belongs to those who are like little children. The ruler is certainly no small child in terms of his physical maturity and his status in the community. He is, after all, a ruler. At first Jesus responds to his use of the adjective "good" in his greeting. Ultimately only God is good, Jesus says. There must be a bit of irony in that statement for Luke's audience, because the point of this whole story thus far is that Jesus himself, as son of God, does deserve that title. Jesus then goes on to list off the fifth through the ninth commandments, those having to do with human treatment of other humans. "You know the commandments: Adultery, murder, stealing, lying, honoring father and mother." It is interesting that Jesus does not include the command that condemns coveting what others have. The ruler can respond with some confidence at that point, "From the time I became accountable for my own actions, I have kept the commandments." He just lacks one thing, Jesus says. "Sell your possessions and distribute to the poor, and you will have treasure in heaven; and come, follow me." We find out why coveting wasn't a problem–he already had it all! But like the people of Noah's day, and the people of Sodom, his identity was all tied up in his possessions. To give everything away would have destroyed his whole social existence. The title of ruler would be gone, the wealth that kept that identity and power would be gone. He would have nothing except that other-worldly notion of "treasure in heaven." Luke gives us this wonderful understatement: "he was sad because he was very rich." Jesus sees him standing there and he goes on. "How hard it is for those who have wealth to enter the kingdom. It is easier for a camel to go through the eye of a sewing needle than for a rich man to enter the reign of God." Once you get connected to the securities and identities of this world, it is too hard to let go.

Those standing there watching and listening cannot believe their eyes and ears. Even the Law taught that wealth was a sign of blessing from God. If this ruler has kept the commandments since he was a kid, and been blessed with wealth and power, and he can't be saved, who can? When the question is, "What shall I do to inherit eternal life?" the response of Jesus is, "It's impossible!" The question itself is a contradiction. Inheritance is always gift, not earned possession. But while humanly impossible to attain, for the rich as well as anyone else, with God salvation is possible. Just as the angel told Mary when he announced that she would have a son, "With God all things are possible," so in this story it is amazing grace that saves, not human effort. We have nothing to bring before God, and the things we do have become our biggest obstacle. The rich ruler could not embrace the new identity of Jesus without forfeiting his social identity that was based on power and possessions. That is the secret to little children belonging to the kingdom! They have nothing to bring except themselves before God. There is no earthly identity established, no collection of rules kept or possessions held. No self-exaltation to overcome.

It is somewhat ironic again, that Peter responds to Jesus with the comment, we have left our homes and followed you. The truth is he and his fellow disciples had left old identities to follow Jesus. There is commendation from Jesus for the losses they have suffered–There is no one who has left house or wife or brothers or parents or children–that's what these guys have done–for the sake of the reign of God, who will not receive manifold more in this time, and in the age to come eternal life. There is blessing in leaving behind the identities and securities of this life for the sake of the kingdom. But there can never be any reliance placed on what we have done or given up. It is this same man, Peter, who soon will deny ever having been associated with Jesus, not once but three times.

How hard it is for a rich man to enter the kingdom of God. In fact, it's humanly impossible, because *we* (not he) we become so attached to our stuff and to the identity that comes from the location of our stuff in relationship to other people and their stuff. Conspicuous consumption has so much to do with identity in our culture, and identity in this church. We all are in the process of conforming to security and values of the culture around us, and there is no escape. Can you imagine God saying to any of us this morning, "One thing you lack; go sell everything you own, and give to the poor, and come follow me." Think of our litany of excuses. Well, he really doesn't mean you have to do that, you just have to be *willing* to do that. Just make sure you could sell that car, you *could* sell that house. *Don't get too emotionally attached.*

No, as long as we are going to earn our way in by our performance, we are all doomed. Only because of God's amazing grace is there hope for any of us. Compared to any other standard of living in the world, we all are rich! To some degree or another we all would be horribly saddened if told to give up our earthly identity in order to inherit eternal life. *Amazing Grace, how sweet the sound. What is impossible with men is possible with God.* There is no escaping the call of discipleship to let go of this life and its passions and power and identity, and follow Jesus. There is no escaping that trip to the cross that Jesus himself must make. We, too, are still called to let go. There are times when I feel so helplessly caught up in this world and this culture, buying more, needing more, trapped in the affluence of Nashville, Tennessee in a lifestyle that I really enjoy and really don't want to give up. But I worship a God who does the impossible. And in his amazing grace I find comfort, and hope, and I see myself for who I really am. I love the verse in the song *Nearer, Still Nearer*: "Nothing I bring, naught as an offering to Jesus my king. Only my sinful my sinful contrite heart."

That is all we bring before God, isn't it? But it is precisely when we can let go of everything else and be that vulnerable and exposed and honest that the impossible becomes possible. Our materialism ought to bother us. Our need to conform to this world ought to bother us. We need to let go, and this morning we cry out, *We believe, help our unbelief!* We want to seek first his kingdom and his righteousness, but it is so easy to want our own little kingdoms.

Who will follow Jesus this morning? Who will go to the cross with him, and die with him in baptism, putting the person who would be king to death so that Christ can be king and Lord of life? Who will become like a child this morning and come to Jesus with nothing but a sinful, contrite heart?

THE FIRST ORDER OF BUSINESS

In April, 1998, four families, with the blessings of their parent congregations, planted the Northpointe Community Church of Christ in a suburb of Detroit. On the second Sunday that they met, with about 40 young and energetic persons in attendance, I delivered the following sermon.

The sermon's content squares with Greg Sterling's exegetical observation that among the synoptics, Luke/Acts has a comparatively strong emphasis on prayer. The Lucan theology of prayer as guidance and as a means of determining God's will is foundational to this particular pericope and sermon. The sermon attempts to accomplish the focus identified by Dean Smith, "It is God at work and not ourselves."

Chapter Seven
Sermons from Acts

D A V I D   F L E E R

FIRST ORDER OF BUSINESS
ACTS 1:6-14

What do you do when you've been given a monster job and little time to do it? You've been elected chair of the PTA. It's your job to raise a quarter million dollars for the computer and software drive…by June 1st. What do you do?

The IRS calls. You're being audited. You'll need to find and organize every receipt for every item you've ever purchased over the last seven years. What do you do?

You've just been promoted and must move to St. Louis. The company isn't dealing with the house. You must sell it this summer! Repairs to attend to: paint the exterior, fix the leaking faucet, spruce up the lawn, trim the shrubs and trees. Don't forget all the stuff in the garage! What do you do?

Do you sense the same kind of urgency in this text: Jesus tells his disciples to be his witnesses to the four corners of the world (1:8) and then he ascends into heaven. He hands the disciples a monster task and then he promptly leaves. That's why their first activity is so surprising: they wait and pray. You'd expect these church planters to be engaged in more useful activity. You'd expect to hear, "Four corners of the world!?! We need to get organized. We need to get ready. We need a strategy!"

The disciples have just been asked by Jesus to be evangelistic: to the Jews first (good) but then to the Samaritans (bad) and finally the Gentiles (worse). That's what Jesus said. You'd expect to hear, "We'll need some meetings to get prepared. All of this foreign work, we'll need to play act, role model, pretend that the room is full of Arab Gentiles." You'd expect someone with foresight to say, "We need to get ready for these people: language study and cross-cultural training."

The disciples are starting a church! They'll need a preacher and a worship leader and greeters. Friendly people, handsome people with name tags for all the visitors.

The disciples are starting a church! They'll need someone in charge of children. What will they do with the kids? Junior Worship? Bible class teachers? Activities? Education coordinator? They have decisions to make and people to take charge. Leaders! Someone in charge of food and someone in charge of money. They'll need a treasurer. Choose carefully. Remember the sorry record of the one who went before.

The disciples are starting a church! In Acts they have good reason to be overwhelmed with urgency because they have business to do. And business they get.

In the second chapter they'll get converts. The baptisms number 3000. They'll need a baptistery! And towels and baptismal gowns. Someone says, "I know a guy who builds portable baptisteries…." There will be 3000 responses. Responses? They'll need a PA system. Will someone be recording Peter's sermon? There is useful activity to do!

The disciples are starting a church and they have business to do. And business they get. By Acts 3 they have a healing. A healing? By Acts 4 there's trouble with the religious leaders… a lawyer? By Acts 5 Annanias and Saphira die. Funeral arrangements!

When the church gets business it naturally feels the need to get busy preparing properly for these opportunities. The first impulse is to prepare with organization and committees and programs and the selection of good leaders. That's why the disciples' response is so surprising. "They devoted themselves to prayer…continually" (1:14). The first thing they do is pray. Amazing!

Jesus' "orders" are to witness to the entire world (1:8) and then he leaves. The first thing they do is pray. Not select. Not organize, Not position themselves. Not rely on their ample resources. Their first task is prayer. The business of the church is prayer. Prayer is our most useful activity.

There exists in the Roman Catholic Church monks and priests whose sole task is to pray. That is their job. "What a waste," some might say. But, who has the vision of the first Christians? When we wait on God and pray we have their vision.

They all relied on God. Everyone of them. They all prayed.

Men and women. The women were not assigned kitchen and child care duties. The men and women gathered to pray. The women had been with Jesus from the beginning, financing his ministry, witnessing his death, burial, and resurrection. Now they are present, waiting, praying, and anticipating the Spirit.

There is one woman present whose name is Mary. She is the mother of Jesus. It was Mary to whom the angel said, "The Holy Spirit will overshadow you" and she gave birth to Jesus. Now she is present just before the descent of the Holy Spirit, which will give birth to the church. Prayer, Luke says, is the job of everyone.

I was once associated with a church that had a tremendous need and knew they had to pray. We all gathered at the building where we tried to divide into groups. Men in one place. Women in another. And, for the progressives, men and women together in a third location. One man said he couldn't pray if he knew of the co-ed pray-ers. A woman said she had a problem that he had a problem, and she couldn't focus on her prayers. What a mess. In Acts 1, they all pray.

This, of course, isn't the only time Luke tells us the early church prayed. When they selected a replacement for Judas, the church prayed. When they heard threats from religious leaders, the church prayed. Before they selected seven men to help the widows, the church prayed. When the Samarians were converted, the church prayed. Before Peter raised Tabitha from the dead, the church prayed. Before Peter was released from prison, the church prayed. Before Paul and Barnabas were sent out on the first missionary journey, the church prayed.

So, when the disciples pray in Acts 1:14 they are beginning what will become a custom. But, this custom wasn't generated by their overwhelming need. This custom of prayer wasn't generated by a preacher wagging a finger at them, commanding, "Pray!" Prayer is a practice they learned from Jesus himself.

Luke carefully records that Jesus prayed during his baptism. Before Jesus selected the twelve, he spent the entire night in prayer. When Jesus' face and clothing were transformed and "became glowing," on the Mount of Transfiguration, Jesus prayed. At the return of the seventy missionaries Jesus prayed. Before Peter's great confession Jesus prayed. Jesus, Luke says, "Would often slip away to the wilderness to pray" (Luke 5:18). Luke says that "Jesus would spend the whole night in prayer"

(6:12). So, after several months of observing Jesus' habit of prayer, the disciples finally requested, "Lord teach us to pray" (Luke 11:1). Evidently Jesus taught his disciples well. Now they are praying, just as Jesus prayed.

When I've taught a course on the early church at Rochester College, I've asked the sophomore students to identify the "marks of the church." The answer I'm hoping to hear is the one found here in the first chapter: prayer. But, the better answer is that this fledgling church in Acts is doing what they've seen Jesus do. Their "mark" is that they are praying...just like Jesus.

So, we're getting started. A new church! What would Jesus do if he were here? Good question. Much better to look to Jesus than to the places we're tempted to look: To the Rochester congregation with its vibrant youth program, or the North Warren and Eastpointe congregations where your friends and family worship, or to Rick Warren's Purpose Driven Church, or to the Kensington Community Church with their remarkable numerical growth. Look back instead to the first church, still fresh from the influence of Jesus, still walking in his shadow. Look closely. What do you see? Do you see them praying, bowing, or prostrate, or with hands raised? And their eyes, not closed but looking intently...back into the Gospel...looking intently at the figure of Jesus, who himself is at prayer. You and I see these first disciples of Christ, deciding to be in his company, like trainees or interns, watching Jesus, doing as he did, becoming like him in prayer.

The first disciples were told to be "witnesses to the end of the earth." Everywhere! Cover the world! You have only so many hours. Get busy? No, pray! These aren't "orders" from above. Jesus encourages us to pray. Jesus said that if earthly parents, who are far from perfect, know how to give good gifts to their children, how much more will our father in heaven give to those who ask. Jesus said, if a judge, who does not fear God nor respect humankind, can grant requests to a petitioning widow, how much more will our father in heaven hear us when we pray. Ask...seek...knock...Jesus said, because God wants to respond! The reason we wait and pray is that we know that the power and wisdom and energy will come from a source far beyond our feeble selves. The reason we pray, said Jesus, is not that "prayer works!" but that God works, God listens, God cares, God acts.

What do you do when you've been given a monster job? This church? This community? This job? This life? The impulse is to start moving, get organized. The answer is to pray. All of us pray. But, pray for what?

When Jesus teaches his disciples to pray in Luke 11, he ends his encouragement with a confusing word. He says, "Pray because God will answer," "pray because God will answer," "Pray because (and now the confusing phrase) God will give the Holy Spirit to those who ask." The Holy Spirit? Where did that come from? I hesitate to admit this, but I've always thought the Holy Spirit was, in light of the context of Luke 11, "out of place." But, in light of Acts 1, the Holy Spirit is exactly what the disciples need, are waiting for, asking for, and exactly what Jesus will send! The Holy Spirit isn't "out of place" for us, the Holy Spirit is exactly what we need. What sounds out of place in our context are bereavement committees and ushers and floral arrangements and welcome cards and contracts, legal disclaimers and PA systems. What we pray for is the power of the Holy Spirit.

We pray because Jesus prayed and encourages us to do the same. The church gathered after Jesus' ascension and prayed for the Holy Spirit. Jesus' encouragement to pray ended with the promise that God would send the Spirit to those who prayed. God answers our prayers and sends the Spirit who forgives us and empowers us and leads us in determining and doing the will of God. The disciples are starting a church and we have business to do. Let us pray!

WHY DO YOU GO TO CHURCH ON SUNDAY?
ACTS 3:1-10

I've attempted to articulate the deeper and more significant reasons for going to church through the juxtaposition of the sermon's pericope (Acts 3:1-10) with the passage that immediately follows: Peter's sermon in 3:11-26. In Acts, Luke often uses a sermon to explain a confusing event (Acts 2:14-36, for example, clarifies the perplexity in 2:5-13 over the descent of the Spirit in 2:1-4). So, Peter's sermon in 3:11-26 throws light on the healing story in 3:1-10.

I've tried to follow Luke's literary lead by using Peter's comment on forgiveness to become the focus for the sermon's conclusion. While the sermon begins with the dubious connection of First Century temple prayer to Twenty first century church attendance, "textual sensitivity" eventually prevails and the sermon examines Luke's focus in connection to our deepest need.

The sermon was preached in May 1999 at the Livonia, Michigan Church of Christ. The congregation had recently suffered through the difficult departure of several disgruntled members.

WHY DO YOU GO TO CHURCH ON SUNDAY?
ACTS 3:1-10

Why do you go to church on Sunday?

"That's a good question" you say. "Let's see…I go to church to worship God. Yes, that's why we all go to church on Sunday."

Why do you go to church on Sunday?

"I go to church on Sunday to be edified," someone else says, citing the passage in Paul that explains the correct motive for attending Sunday services.

Edification and worship are the correct answers to the question, "Why do you go to church on Sunday?"

Let's be more specific, Why do you go to church on Sunday?

"More specific? The answer, I guess, is either because of the singing or the prayers or the sermon, or the Lord's Supper. Or the answer is…fellowship."

What do you think of these answers?

What do you think of these answers:

"I go to church out of habit. It's a good habit, like brushing teeth. I go to church because ever since I was a little boy my parents went to church and instilled the habit in me."

Or this…" I go to church as a long term investment. I have in mind my children and my marriage. Sunday School functions as a support system for our beliefs. The adults are like an extended family for the kids. My husband and I need positive models of couples who desire and work on staying together. Church is the best investment in family that we know."

Or this… "I go to church to meet people. I mean good people. I'm honestly looking for folks who have morals. People you can trust. It seems that church is the best place to find those kind of people."

Or this … "I go to church so I can feel good about my day. If Sunday starts out with church instead of sleep or the paper and coffee, it's a better day. It works!"

Or this… "I go to church because one Sunday when I was little as I was sitting in church with the sun through the stained glass windows beaming into the sanctuary…it was just after communion… and I was sitting between my grandparents and mom, and the congregation was singing what has become my favorite hymn …at that precise moment I felt a warm, compelling, and spiritual awakening. I've never had the same feeling again. But, I keep going to church hoping that one day I'll feel it again."

Or, what do you think of these answers:

"You want me to be dead honest? I go to church because I'm in real estate and church is the place where I cultivate my business. I'll be straight. Church is a place where I make money. Church people are my best customers. I just wish this church were a little bigger!"

Or this… "I'm here to find a wife. There's bars and there's churches. There's better women in churches than in taverns."

Why do you go to church on Sunday?

What do you think of this answer? [read Acts 3:1-10]

The lame man went to the temple gate looking for some money. Silver and gold. Marks. Crowns. Francs. Dollars. He went to the temple gate to enhance his collection of famous Americans, especially Benjamin Franklin! The lame man went to the Temple gate for motives "beneath" the ones articulated in Scripture: worship and edification. What he got was something he had not anticipated!

There is a lot of unanticipated activity in this story. The lame man came for money and was healed. That wasn't anticipated!

Peter and John were going to the temple to pray and then, something they had not anticipated, they performed a miracle!

Religious leaders thought Jesus' power and influence had died. Then something they had not anticipated: the once scattered disciples were filled with his power.

Even the crowd: they knew the man was crippled and begged at the Temple gate. They did not anticipate him to move by his own legs.

Back to the question we asked. I know of people who have gone to church for mixed reasons. Divorced: a single mother looking for a hand or a shoulder. Alcoholic: looking for a sober, firm and understanding voice. Friendless: looking for a pal. Broke: looking for a meal. They all come to church with broken lives and broken hearts. Emotionally lame, they limp into church. Spiritually lame, they drag into service. And, frankly, they don't have high expectations. The single mother will settle for a free baby sitter one hour a week while she dutifully sits through a Bible class. The friendless man will settle for two or three handshakes and a courteous, "good morning."

What is Luke saying in this story? I get the impression that the focus is on us, the lame man at the temple gate. The spotlight seems to be on you and me. Notice the unusual quantity of words Luke employs in 3:8, "[the lame man] leaped…stood…walked…entered…[he was] walking… leaping." There is so much activity, it looks like a Red Wings game. Where is the focus of activity? Where's the puck? I see it! I see the lame man. I see you and me. With all of those descriptive words, Luke seems to put the focus on the lame man, or us.

Then again, Peter appears to be the one getting all the attention. After all, he is doing the miracle. That's what the crowd and the religious leaders think.

Then again, maybe we are to be impressed by the crowd. Consider all the action words they get in 3:9-10. They "saw" and "took note" and were "filled with amazement." Maybe we are to fix our eyes on the crowd. Luke has been keeping attendance, counting converts since the 3000 baptisms on Pentecost.

When Peter gets the undo attention from the crowd he tells us who is the story's focus. Listen to him: "In the name of Jesus," he says (3:6), "By the power of Jesus," he explains in his sermon (3:16). "In the name of Jesus," he tells the religious leaders (4:7,10) the miracle took place.

The problem is, we didn't see God do it during the story. We were so caught up with the reaction of the crowd, or the language of Peter, or the immediate response of the man once lame, that we missed the passive wording of Luke, "and his ankles were strengthened." Peter clarifies for us, three times he says Jesus did it (3:6), Jesus did it (3:16), Jesus did it (4:10). Now we know who did the miracle.

Suppose it's true that you get what you came for. Looking for better children and that's what you get. Looking for a better marriage and that's what you get. Looking for a better day and that's what you get. Looking for a better feeling and that's what you get. Looking for more customers and that's what you get. Looking for a better husband and that's what you get. Looking for better friends and that's what you get. These and other wants and desires may well be satisfied in church.

But, what God is after…more than a shoulder or a hand or a pocket full of potential customers or room full of good influence…What God is after is a need even deeper than these needs. What God is after is what is done for this man through Peter, done "in the name of Jesus." This phrase, "in the name of Jesus" has been soiled by the televangelists. But, "in the name of Jesus" is Luke's phrase and he uses it with intention. Luke says "the name of Jesus" at the crucial moments in his story. At baptism people receive forgiveness of sins "in the name of Jesus"(2:38); Samarians receive the forgiveness of sins "in the name of Jesus"(8:16); Cornelius receives the forgiveness of sins "in the name of Jesus"(10:48); the Ephesians receive the forgiveness of sins "in the name of Jesus"(19:5). The man's need, his greatest need is met "in the name of Jesus."

I knew a couple who were members of our local congregation. They had suffered long over an affair she had had two decades before and two states away. He could not come to forgive her. The most basic need they had could not be met.

On the other hand, I knew a married man, struggling with his sexual preferences, came forward in a church that received him and forgave him and accepted him. His most basic need was met, "in the name of Jesus."

This story of ours begins with Peter and John going to the Temple to pray. It ends with the church at prayer. The leaders of the religious community didn't take well to the healing and especially the preaching about Jesus. The leaders threatened the disciples of Jesus. Threatened to kill them if they continued to preach Jesus. The church responded by asking God…not for revenge…not to remove the threat…but for boldness! That's how this story ends! It ends with Christians living for something larger than themselves. And, listen to this: "in the name of Jesus" believers in Christ were willing to suffer (5:41), risk their lives "in the name of Jesus"(15:26), and die "in the name of Jesus" because they have something they live for that is larger than themselves.

Why do you come to church? Most of us are here for reasons somewhere between the biblically correct but thoughtless reason and the outright base and manipulative motive. We are here looking for something. We are searching for relationship: friends or extended family. We are hungry for a good feeling or a spiritual moment.

We also come to church struggling with the realities of our imperfect lives: our personality defects, our sins. We come full of it: bitterness and short fuses with long memories and the knowledge of others' failures. Then we sit next to our spouse or across from the one we can not forgive and we hear, "On the night in which he was betrayed, Jesus took the cup and said "...father forgive them for they don't know what they do." We come to church and we pray, "Our father in heaven, forgive us our sins as we forgive those who sin against us." We come to church and have the significant opportunity, "in the name of Jesus," to forgive and be forgiven.

Whatever your motive, whatever your understanding, may God take you, "in the name of Jesus" and, as He did with the characters in Luke's story, give you something to live for that is larger than yourself and deeper than any need you can articulate, "in the name of Jesus."

WHAT DO YOU THINK OF THE CONVERSION OF SAUL OF TARSUS?

Sermonic form blends the Bible with contemporary society in the following sermon. The sermon begins with current and obvious reactions to Saul's conversion but slowly evolves into natural reactions suggested from the biblical text. The form of the sermon thus creates a perspective from which to hear the text. Allowing congregational fears to be articulated through the resistance of Ananias, the text and sermon function as a prophetic word to encourage the congregation to accept and celebrate biblical and modern day conversions of Saul of Tarsus.

The sermon was preached in 1998, during the first months of the existence of the Northpointe Community Church of Christ.

WHAT DO YOU THINK OF THE CONVERSION OF SAUL OF TARSUS?
ACTS 9:1-19

What do you think of the conversion of Saul of Tarsus?

"I'm all for it," you say. "Saul/Paul is one of my favorite writers. Why, I've memorized several of his passages. Listen to this, 'I can do all things through Christ who strengthens me.' Or this, 'The wages of sin is death.' I love his stuff on the Lord's Supper."

What do you think of the conversion of Saul of Tarsus?

"I'm all for it," you say. "I love his attitude: loving but firm. That's what I like. What he says in Galatians, "If anyone should preach a Gospel other than what he heard from me…let him be accursed."

What do you think of the conversion of Saul of Tarsus?

"I'm all for it," you say. "Paul is so smart. I'm still trying to figure out what he's saying in Romans 9-11. Paul may be the smartest Christian ever. I'm glad he became a Christian. We need intelligent Christians like Paul."

What do you think of the conversion of Saul of Tarsus?

"I'm all for it," you say. "I think we have his story here in Acts 9 for the same reason we have other conversion stories in Acts: to show us what we must do to be saved. You know, faith repentance and baptism. It's all here. Yes, I'm all for the conversion of Saul of Tarsus."

What do you suppose Luke thinks of the conversion of Saul of Tarsus?

Luke has told us that Saul is the persecutor of the church. In fact in his two volume account, nearly every other time Luke uses the verb for persecute he uses it with reference to Saul. Luke has painted the portrait of the enemy of Christ and the church and the face of the enemy is Saul.

Perhaps you've known converts whose previous life looked a lot like Saul of Tarsus. I have a colleague at Rochester College who claims that he was a real rogue before he became a Christian. He had no goals except to drive fast German sports cars and chase women. Rogue, yes, but no Saul of Tarsus.

I knew another man who before he converted to Christ was a "no account" hippie. At the 1968 National Democratic Convention he threw molotov cocktails out the window of his

Volkswagen bug. He later converted and became a minister in Colorado. A radical conversion, yes. But he was no Saul of Tarsus. Neither of these men were persecutors of Christians, as Luke pictures Saul.

Saul was "public enemy number one." The first time we meet Saul it is at the murder of Stephen. Luke says the execution squad "laid their robes at the feet of Saul." He says, "At the feet of Saul." Like the church placing funds "at the feet of the apostles," Luke pictures Saul as the one in authority. Saul is in charge of the murder. Saul was not the coat check man. He was the ringleader, the mastermind of the murder.

The next time we see Saul, he is leading a campaign to terrorize the followers of Jesus (8:1-3). We later read that Saul is "breathing threats and murder" against Christians.

How do you feel about the conversion of Saul of Tarsus? This is not the conversion of your friendly neighbor across the street, the man who collects the mail when you leave town, or the kindly woman who watches your children on Friday evenings. Saul is not the nice neighbor who bakes brownies and brings them to your kitchen for no apparent purpose. Saul is not among the persons of whom you have said, "He'd make a great Christian. Why, he is patient and kind and loving and joyful and good and gentle. It seems like he already has the fruit of the Holy Spirit." No, Saul is not the friendly neighbor whom you'd love to see at church.

How do you feel about the conversion of Saul of Tarsus? Luke says that Saul was a persecutor of Christians and he tells us exactly what that entailed. Saul "ravaged" the church like an animal on the prowl, violating Christians by entering uninvited into their homes or church meetings and then dragging them out for imprisonment or murder (8:1-2).

How do you feel about the conversion of Saul of Tarsus? Listen to the testimony of the women and men and children who suffered under Saul's reign of terror. "Frankly, it makes me mad," one survivor says. "I lost my sister to that zealot. He imprisoned her. Then he had her killed." Or, "My best friend quit Christianity out of fear for Saul of Tarsus." Or, "Saul terrorized our congregation for months. When I hear his name I still become physically ill."

How do you feel about the conversion of Saul of Tarsus? Perhaps we should ask the one Christian in Luke's account. Ask

Ananias. Ananias' concern when told that Saul was a candidate for conversion, expressed the very sentiments we'd have felt. "You want *this* guy?" (9:13-14). Ananias gives voice to our objections. "Not Saul!" we'd say, "Punish him! If you're going to convert someone, convert my neighbor. Look, here she comes now with brownies and milk for the children." How do you feel about the conversion of Saul of Tarsus? Of course Ananias protests, and so do we!

How do you feel about the conversion of Saul of Tarsus? Perhaps we should ask the man himself. Ask the one who was transformed from persecutor to apostle, one of history's most stunning and inexplicable turnabouts. He never forgot. He seems never to have lost sight of having tortured the body of Christ. To the Corinthians he later wrote, "and last of all, as to one untimely born, He appeared to me also." To the Galatians he later wrote, "You have heard of my former manner of life–how I used to persecute the church of God without measure and tried to destroy it." To the Philippians he said, "I was a persecutor of the church." To Timothy he wrote, "Of sinners, I am foremost." That's what he thought of his conversion!

As you begin to work in this community, I wonder what God has in store. I can imagine there may be a few Sauls of Tarsus. Is it hard to envision a modern day Saul of Tarsus? Since Madelyn Murray O'Hair turned up missing a few years back, the church hasn't felt an "old fashioned" threat to close down operations, as with Saul of Tarsus. Of course, we've created a few enemies of the church. Look for them in the coming election literature. The usual suspects: abortion, casinos, gambling, and homosexuality. These "issues" and the persons who surround them are portrayed as the enemies of the church today. What would you think of the conversion of Saul of Tarsus, in their case? God comes into the life of the serious gambler, the homosexual, the pro-choice advocate. Why is it hard to envision a modern day Saul of Tarsus? I imagine a young woman with one or two children looking for help. I imagine a single man recently divorced and lonely. I imagine someone who at this moment is alcoholic, or is taking drugs, who this morning is not in the pew but on the couch nursing a hangover. I imagine people who are caught up in sin. I imagine teens with violent desires and goals. I imagine homosexuals. I imagine irresponsible mothers. I imagine abusive husbands. I imagine a community full of Saul of Tarsuses.

How do you feel about the conversion of Saul of Tarsus? What do you suppose God thought of the conversion of Saul? God is quoted on the matter. "Go," God said, "for he is a chosen instrument of mine to carry my name before the Gentiles and kings and the sons of Israel" (9:15-16). Which is exactly what happened. Saul changed his name to Paul and carried the gospel to the Gentiles, even speaking to King Aggrippa and hoping to do the same before Caesar. Evidently, God approved of the converion of Saul of Tarsus.

As you begin to work in this community, I wonder what God has in store. I can imagine there may be a few Sauls of Tarsus. I imagine you as Ananias. And when asked what you think of the conversion of this man or that woman will likely feel what Annanais felt when told of Saul. Likely you'll feel what Matthew, James, John, and the other apostles felt when they first heard (8:26). You'd like to run or hide or just hope they would head down the street to that other church that seems so well equipped to handle people like...Saul of Tarsus. You'll want to put a sign outside our building that reads "White collar, upwardly mobile, perfumed, with well behaved children, scratch golfers, with homes that resemble the value of ours: Welcome!" But you know what is right. You know that if God had a purpose for Saul he has a purpose for persons on the bottom of your "want to convert" list. God has a purpose for the offensive men and women who will become Christians and worship here. Does he not have a purpose for you?

"What do you think of the conversion of Saul of Tarsus?" is to ask what you think of the conversion of the most notorious enemy of the church and what you think of the possibility of welcoming and baptizing everyone into this church.

"What do you think of the conversion of Saul of Tarsus?" We respond by telling the truth. "Yes," we say, "We are in favor of the conversion of Saul of Tarsus, on this day, in this community, in this church. So, help us, God."

GOD GIVES SECOND CHANCES

In this sermon I enact the preacher's and congregation's struggle against the strong temptation to impose our issues ("why me") on a particular text. Once the sermon gives way to the text, its focal point emerges from Luke's literary allusions to a prior narrative in his two volume work. Except for his cameo appearance at the Jerusalem council (Acts 15), Peter's prison escape (in Acts 12) is his final act on Luke's stage. In this context, Luke's historical references, grammar, and other linguistic tools draw readers back to Peter's denial.[1]

Echoes of Dean Smith's concern for Jesus' role as intercessor[2] are found in the refrain of the sermon's second half, "Jesus prays for us!" I've used the phrase stylistically and as an obvious reminder of Peter's (and our) only hope for faithfulness: Jesus' interceding prayer. This sermon was delivered at the Northpointe Community Church of Christ, Spring, 1998 during its first few months of existence.

---

[1] For additional references, see Luke Timothy Johnson, *The Acts of the Apostles, Sacra Pagina*, Daniel Harrington, ed. (Collegeville, MN: Liturgical Press, 1992), 209-219. In the sermon I mention only a few of the details Johnson identifies.

[2] See above, Dean Smith, "We Will Pray: Preaching About Prayer in Luke-Acts." 80-92.

GOD GIVES SECOND CHANCES
ACTS 12:1-17

Don't you love this story? It is so funny! There are some jolly moments in this narrative! You've got to love the lightheartedness of Rhoda at the gate (12:16). She leaves Peter knocking at the door while the debate rages over whether Rhoda saw Peter or not. Isn't that hilarious! I think it funny the way the angel treats Peter, like a child (12:8). "Put on your shoes. Don't forget your coat," instructs the angel, just like a parent scolding a kindergartner. Or, how about the moment Peter realizes, at the end of his escape, that he is not dreaming (12:11). He's been up for who knows how long and suddenly it occurs to him he is not asleep. That's funny.

There are different levels of humor, too. An angel gets Peter out of jail against incredible odds: chains, bars, and double guards. But Peter can't get through the gate because he's mistaken for an angel. Heh, heh. Or, this chapter begins with Herod wanting to harm the church and ends with Herod eaten by worms. Ha ha. Or, this section of Luke's story begins with one church leader killed and the chief spokesman jailed but ends with the spokesman escaping, the tyrant dead, and the church growing. Ho ho ho.

The humor's fine but where I stall in hearing this story is in the first two verses. My mind's eye keeps going back to James' death. Peter escaped, why not James? Why wasn't James spared? Why did James have to die? I can imagine myself as James' brother or father. Why my brother? Why my son? I can imagine the big celebration after Peter gets into the house. Peter behind the microphone, "I'd like to thank all of you who prayed…God certainly answers prayer!…I would like to thank those of you who never gave up…I'd like to thank my wife …Martha, stand up, honey…Our son, little Peter…come up here, Pete …Daddy's home, little buddy." I look over at James' son, little Jimmy, and James' wife and friends and I say, "Why not James? Why wasn't James spared?"

I'm rehearsing a tune you and I know quite well, "Why me?" We hum it often. In fact, "Why me?" is the recurring refrain in a song I've recently composed. It goes like this:

The basement leaks,
And so does the roof,
The dryer's out,
And I feel like a goof.
Why me? Why me?
The car won't run,
The house needs painting,
I'm out of money,
And my body's fainting.
Why me? Why me?

Peter's house is twice the size of mine. He drives two BMWs and is wintering in Bermuda. Why not me?

There are a lot of people who are seriously asking "Why me?" The parents of the two teenagers…Wait! Stop! Do you see what I'm doing to this text? I've pried this story open with a crow bar and crawled in to stare at my navel. This isn't Luke's perspective, at least not in this story. Luke is telling another tale, and perhaps we should quiet our worries and silence our songs.
"The oven won't work
The dishwasher, too.
Molds in the basement
And, I'm feeling blue…" shhhhh.

Luke doesn't focus on little Jimmy and Mrs. James. His picture is bigger and different. James and Peter are both victims. The Roman government, in the person of Herod Agrippa, is the victimizer. Herod is an evil man and he is after Christians, all of us. This is a story about God's working in our lives, God working against the forces of evil in the life of the church.

Peter's escape, by the way, is Peter's last major appearance in Luke's two volume work. Luke has focused on Peter before. You remember Peter, the fisherman who, after a mammoth catch of fish, "left everything" to follow Jesus. You remember Peter, who tried to walk on water but, "seeing the wind, he became afraid and cried, 'Lord, save me.'" You remember Peter, who was with Jesus on the mount of transfiguration and said something, "not realizing what he was saying." You remember Peter, who was asked by Jesus, "Who do you say that I am?" to which Peter gave the correct response, "You are the Christ of God." You best remember Peter, however, at his most notorious moment. You remember that Peter claimed, "though all may deny you I will never…," denied Jesus three times.

Now the story in Acts 12 is Peter's good-bye appearance, his swan song. And, Luke uses a lot of literary allusions to remind us of Peter's early failure, to remind us specifically of Peter's lowest moment, his worst defeat during the trial of Jesus. Listen to the innumerable references to Peter's nadir moment, his denial of Jesus. Peter, like Jesus, was imprisoned during the Passover. They laid hands on Peter, just as Luke records about Jesus. Peter was arrested, delivered over, and led forth, the exact terms used during Jesus' trial and Peter's denial. There's more. After Jesus rose from the dead, the event was announced by two figures identified as angels. Just before Peter is scheduled for execution an angel tells him to "rise." When the resurrected Jesus appears in the community, they "disbelieve for joy." What a strange phrase. When Peter gets to the house, Rhoda does not open the gate "for joy." The community of believers initially thinks that Peter is a ghost. Some think that Rhoda has seen Peter's angel. The story in Acts 12 is Peter's swan song. Luke's overwhelming literary allusions to Peter's failure during the trial of Jesus is unmistakable.

So, why all of the allusions to Peter's earlier denial? What is Luke telling us? Certainly Luke is saying that the story of Jesus continues through his followers. But there is more here. The arrest. The threat of death. Even the servant girl causes us to recall Peter's worst failure: when he denied Jesus three times. But this is a different Peter. Not without sin, like some saint, but victorious in a situation that has all the details of his previous failure. This is no coincidence. Peter's last story parallels his worst story. Luke presents Peter's last appearance in the same context as his worst experience.

So, what allowed Peter to conquer his weakest moment? How did the second chance not become just another slot in the downward spiral of his failure? Perhaps you'll remember Jesus' words to Peter on the night he was denied. Do you remember? Jesus said, "Satan has demanded permission to sift you like wheat; but I have prayed for you, that your faith may not fail." Jesus prayed for him!

God is a God of second chances. And, like Peter, in this congregation we are people who have failed. In marriage, divorced. In parenting, abuse. In communication, lies. In acquiring what we need, greed. Then, into your life comes the grace of God, forgiveness. Penitent like Peter who wept bitterly after hearing the cock crow, perhaps you have experienced spiritual renewal and God's grace. Jesus said, "I have prayed for you, that your faith may not fail." Jesus prayed for him! God is a God of second chances!

Perhaps for you there will come opportunity when God will give you a second chance. Into your life will appear the same situations as before, when you failed. The same people, the same sounds, the same smells. Only this time instead of bowing to temptation you'll experience victory. Perhaps once under the curse of alcohol you'll find someone battling the same demon that once haunted you. Outside the same bar, holding your once favorite drink, even with the friends with whom you once drank. This is no "deja vu," this is God giving you another opportunity. Jesus said, "I have prayed for you, that your faith may not fail." Jesus prays for you! Victory! God is a God of second chances!

Perhaps as a child you suffered abuse: verbal, emotional, physical, sexual. Now, as a parent, you have opportunity to break the cycle and offer good love to replace the vortex of pain. Jesus prays for you! God is a God of second chances. Maybe for you it has been greedy acquisition. Now God gives you opportunity for a life of integrity. Jesus prays for you! God is a God of second chances!

Rhoda, the servant girl, comes to the gate. The last servant girl, you remember, to have associated with Peter, "looked intently at him, and then told those gathered around the fire, 'This man was with Jesus, too.'" Peter denied her claim, "Woman, I do not know him." A lot has happened since then. Repentance has happened. Bitter weeping has happened since then. Forgiveness has happened. Grace has happened. Jesus has prayed for him.

I recall, from a previous ministry, a work the congregation did to help those recovering from the emotional ravages of divorce. We identified a need and invited a speaker from Colorado to come speak to our group. People invited their divorced neighbors and divorced bankers and divorced grocery clerks and divorced friends. And they all came! For our opening session we had the fellowship hall packed with divorced people. In came our speaker. We went cheap. This church had little budget for this kind of work. So we found someone who charged airfare and lunch. We got what we paid for, I thought, when I discovered, to my horror, that our featured speaker had a discernible and distracting stutter. He was painful to hear...for me. But not for every other person in the group. The speaker had what the people needed to hear. He'd been divorced. He knew the pain and spoke with the integrity of having lived through the heartbreak of rejection and failure. God had given him a second chance. And the divorced truck drivers and the divorced bankers and the divorced school teachers all listened and cried as they heard how God had forgiven and healed. Like Peter, our speaker modeled the hope of victory in the second chance. Jesus prays for us! God is a God of second chances!

If we were to take a poll and ask with which New Testament character do we best identify, Peter would win the poll every time. Why? Because of his sinfulness and honesty, probably. If that is true, we also identify with Peter because we want victory in the second opportunity. We long to have Jesus pray for us and experience victory in the very setting of our worst defeat.

This is no story for self absorbed baby boomers who are obsessed with navel gazing, asking, "why me?" Nor does this story find relief in the lightness of the occasion, the humor of funny, funny Rhoda. No! This is a story for those who remember Peter, to whom Jesus said, "Satan has demanded permission to sift you like wheat; but I have prayed for you, that your faith may not fail." This is the story where God uses Peter, as he will use you, even in the ugliest scenes of your life, to have victory over the sins that once claimed you. He told Peter he would pray for him. Jesus prayed for him! Jesus prays for you! That is the power of God. Through the power of God, with his second chance, may you experience God's forgiveness and victory!

THE BATTLE FOR YOUR SOUL

The following sermon was delivered to undergraduate students at the Rochester College chapel during the first week of classes for Fall semester, 1998. I invite the audience into the "real world" of Acts where evil is incarnate and the Church resists through reliance upon the power of God's Holy Spirit. The sermon works under the assumption that Scripture better understands and reveals our condition than do we. To allow for a hearing of the text, I first dismiss the cartoonish depictions of the devil – images that ignore or pacify our concerns. The sermon gives Luke opportunity to help us imagine the horrific one who tempts individuals and communities to abandon hope.

THE BATTLE FOR YOUR SOUL
ACTS 13:1-12

The story just read is a clip from a larger tale of Jesus and his second incarnation, the church. This story is one of empowerment by the Holy Spirit who speaks to and sends Paul and Barnabas out of Antioch and on a mission. It is also a story of confrontation with evil powers. As soon as the Spirit launches the mission team, evil arrives to abort their project. The culprit's name is Bar Jesus (a.k.a. Elymas). The title Paul gives him is more descriptive: he is "the devil's son."

The empowerment of the Holy Spirit is met with obstruction from the devil. This isn't the first time, nor the last, that this has happened. Do you remember the story of Jesus' baptism as told by Luke? At the beginning of his ministry Jesus was baptized in the Jordan River. Then, the Spirit descended upon him like a dove. Jesus was full of the Holy Spirit, Luke tells us, when he left the river for the wilderness, "to be tempted by the devil." The die is cast. The Holy Spirit comes into the house and the devil slips through the door.

Do you remember Luke's description of the day of Pentecost? The Spirit descended upon Peter and the twelve and by the end of Acts 4 Peter told Annanias and Saphira that "Satan has filled your heart." The Holy Spirit comes into the house and the devil slips through the door.

Do you remember how Luke later tells us that when God reached new ground in Samaria and Peter and John came to impart the Holy Spirit that Simon the Sorcerer challenged the Spirit, asking to buy the ability to impart the gift. Peter told him, "To Hell with your money! And you along with it."[3] The Holy Spirit comes into the house and the devil slips through the door.

Do you see the pattern Luke has developed? It continues to this day. The Holy Spirit comes, is active, and then the devil goes to work. For Luke, as often can be said for us, the world is a place of clear choices: black or white, right or wrong, good or evil. It may be the Lord or it may be the devil. For Luke, as with us, if you put everything into a big kettle and boil it down, what you have left is good versus evil. In Luke's account there are

---

[3]Acts 8, Eugene H. Peterson, *The Message: The New Testament in Contemporary Language*, (Colorado Springs: Navpress, 1993).

Christians proclaiming Jesus ...and religious leaders trying to stop them. In Luke's account James and Peter are imprisoned (they're victims)...and Herod who orchestrates the evil (he is the victimizer). In Luke's account God is at work through the Holy Spirit... and the devil retaliates. In Luke's world, as in ours, what it all boils down to is a battle between the forces of good and the forces of evil. Where truth is told opposition arises in an evil and ugly way. So it is here in our story. The Holy Spirit speaks and directs and empowers, and immediately there is a confrontation with evil.

Consider the thick irony of our religious tradition. We've had a rough time with this passage. What's made it rough are all of these references to the Holy Spirit! Listen to the text! In 13:2 the Spirit is talking! We have been very uncomfortable with, "The Spirit said..."

"What? Are you hearing voices?"

Then, in 13:4 the Spirit is sending missionaries out.

"Tell us again why you're going to Panama..."

"The Holy Spirit told us."

"Yeah, right," [eyes rolling with a mocking smile]. We've worried, "This Holy Spirit activity can be taken to such extremes!" In our tradition, we are not used to this kind of language. In our tradition, we are not used to this kind of reality.

But, in Luke's world, the Spirit of God has a direct and active role in the life of the church. In Luke's world the Holy Spirit takes the initiative. We might be surprised and uneasy but that's how it is in Luke's story. In Luke's world, when the church moves, they are following the Spirit's lead. From the preaching on Pentecost to the conversion of Gentiles, in Luke's world, the Spirit acts and the church responds. Always.

In our world we are a bit leery of the Holy Spirit because of the improper emphasis made by the dancing, jumping, fainting, forehead slapping, big haired televangelists. Rightly so. But, the abusers of the Spirit make no comment on Luke's world or on God. Oh, to live in Luke's world.

What we will find, in Luke's world, is that the presence and power of God in our lives is a great relief given the reality of evil. Who can be uncomfortable with the Spirit when the devil is at work?

There is a devil. So, where does this evil one work? Take some cues from Luke's story. In the earlier tale of Simon the Sorcerer, as in this story of Elymas, and later in Acts (19:19), we discover that one of the devil's favorite haunts is in the world of magic. Luke takes it seriously. Magic is off limits for Luke.

Soon after I became a Christian I had opportunity to hear another convert to Christianity, a former spiritualist medium, Ben Alexander. On a fall evening, in Eastern Washington, in a grade school auditorium, with leaves rustling outside, about forty of us gathered to sit on metal folding chairs to hear Ben Alexander's story of his former life as a Spiritualist Medium. After telling of the dark sin in his doings as a medium and in the midst of warnings that we avoid all semblances of evil (especially Ouija boards, tarot cards and seances), the lights in the auditorium went out. Heart beat rates doubled and goose bumps grew large as we sat in thick darkness. Our speaker broke the silence and calmly ordered us out to our cars and off to home. Twenty five years have passed since that autumn night and I've never been tempted to buy a pack of tarot cards and can safely say that I'll never allow a Ouija board in my house!

In our world, however, it's obvious that the devil has diversified. Long ago the devil auctioned off his red suit, pitchfork, and pointed tail. Some Halloween marketing firm acquired the rights. The devil instead has become much more sophisticated and continues to be present and active in this world: in business, in government, in law, on college campuses, secular and Christian, and in your lives. Lest he scare you off he does not approach you like a used car dealer, "For your soul I will give you…" That wouldn't work. Why, you'd rise up and say, "For my soul? Ha! You can't have my soul." Rather, the devil deals this way: he shows you what you want to see. He shows you the kingdoms of the world. He shows you the power and the glory. He shows you fame and fortune. He shows you the lust of the flesh and the lust of the eyes. And once you've begun salivating and say, "That's exactly what I want," the deal is closed. Your soul is in the devil's possession.

The devil is at war in our lives. Watch how the devil works through Elymas who tries to prevent Sergias Paulus from finding meaning in Jesus Christ. At the moment the proconsul desires to hear the missionaries, the devil's advocate works his opposition, he tries to keep Sergias Paulus from finding what he longs for. Don't think for a moment that the devil wishes for you or anyone to find meaning and purpose in life. The devil does not want you to experience hope or acceptance or kindness. The devil does not want you or anyone to channel nurturing or direction or love. Some friends ask you to join in a Bible study or attend a church service or work at the Pontiac Rescue Mission or distribute food and coats at Detroit's Cass Corridor. When the Holy Spirit goes to work in you, expect some kind of devilish interference. The Holy Spirit comes into the house and the devil slips through the door.

The powers of the devil are real. Luke doesn't dress Elymas like Merlin the Magician and expose him as a fake. Luke doesn't walk on stage and grab Merlin's robe and say, "Ha! A rabbit out of a hat? Look where it comes from! Acoin out of thin air? I'll show you how he does it! Cards appearing from nowhere? They're up his sleeve! And, here's how he pretends to saw the lady in half." Luke does not draw the devil's advocate like a cartoon character.

In Luke, the magicians are not entertainers. Luke admits that they have power. Real power! He claims, however, that in every confrontation, the Holy Spirit's power is greater. Remember now the words of Jesus, "Greater is he who is in you than he who is in the world." That's the saving promise in Luke's world and in ours.

We're hearing Luke's story as individuals, probably because we've been trained to hear the Bible as individuals. But this text also speaks to the community's expansion and the community's struggle against the powers of evil. The devil does not specialize exclusively on individuals. He's always worked in the community. He's always worked in society at large.

"Where?" you ask.

Here's one example. Recently, the city of Detroit supported the construction of casinos to help recover the city's economy. For some time we have supported the use of lotteries to fund the construction of roads and education. Or, so we're told. If it's true, then we have welfare moms paying a voluntary tax on the poor! The first weekend it opened, MGM Grand in Detroit reported nearly $50 million in earnings. That translates into $50 million in losses for the gamblers. The casino reported massive winnings because there were lots and lots and lots of losers. For the people with little hope of investing in mutual funds or ending the year with a five figure bonus, spending money on lottery tickets is seen as the only way out. A cafeteria worker budgets $50 a week for lottery tickets saying, "Most people don't need to gamble because they already got the money." And just who do the state's lotteries target in their annual half billion dollar budget? People of color and the poor. Look around! Notice the poor and black neighborhoods of Detroit and Baltimore and Chicago and Buffalo. Lottery outlets on every street corner. But, in the posh white collar wealthy neighborhoods, hardly an outlet. Why? Gambling through casinos and lotteries target the poor. They want the poor's food money, the poor's college money, the poor's electricity money all thrown at Powerball.

"That's their problem," you say. Think again. In his first sermon recorded in Luke, in his inaugural address, Jesus lined up with the poor. Guess where the devil went. God makes it clear that He is always on the side of the poor.

The interests of the devil have long been revealed and the powers of the devil are still real. Luke doesn't expose the devil and his advocates as fake. There are no rabbits under their skirt. In Luke, magicians have power. So, when someone organizes a little "subversive recreation," a student spending trip to the new Motor City Casino, don't expect to find horns growing in the organizer's scalp. But, know this: he is the devil's son. The devil works against you and against institutions and against people groups. The Holy Spirit comes into the house and the devil slips through the door.

But, listen to the promise. After forty days in the wilderness, Jesus defeated the devil. When evil entered Annanias and Saphira, the devil lost. When the devil worked through Simon the Sorcerer, he was invited back to Hell. When Paul confronts the devil's son, Elymas, Elymas scrambles off blind and Sergius Paulus believed in Jesus' power to defeat evil.

This is a new school year. And the Spirit of God, we say, is present. Then, so is the power of evil. The devil, is up to his old tricks and some new ones, too. The battle is for your soul.

As the battle rages, remember again the words of Jesus, "Greater is he who is in you than he who is in the world." That's a promise. Be not leery of the Holy Spirit. Expect to do battle with the devil in sophisticated but not surprising ways. Expect victory. We know this: as it was for Peter, so it will be for you. As it was for Paul, so it will be for you. As it was in Luke's world, so it will be in your world. As it was for Jesus so it will be for you. Jesus sent the Spirit. Jesus promises you, in the struggle, through the Holy Spirit's power, victory.

COMMON GROUND:
LOOKING FOR CONVERSATION PARTNERS

Scholars have debated whether Paul was on trial in Athens, thus demanding a judicial genre of discourse or if he was engaging in "friendly inquiry," thus demanding speech in deliberative form. I find strongest evidence weighing toward discourse aiming to persuade an audience to belief rather than to free the orator from judicial punishment (the prior fate of Socrates amidst the Areopagus). Thus, the following sermon is based on an understanding that Paul was attempting to persuade his Athenian audience to believe.

The sermon is a plea to address our culture as deftly as Paul did his. You may find the sermon "coming up short," with too little to say about how Jesus transforms culture. To this fair critique I look for exegetical support to Luke's conclusion, the ambiguous response to Paul's efforts in Greece. In contrast to the strong reaction to Paul's limited message in Lystra (Acts 14:8-18), Athens provides muted response to a detailed sermon in a lively setting.

I delivered this sermon in April, 1999 at the Twenty sixth annual Michigan State Lectureship, a conference for African American Churches of Christ in Detroit, Michigan.

Certain cities call to mind specific ideals and images. For example, when you hear Washington, D.C., visions of government or power probably come to mind. When I say Fort Knox you think gold bricks and money. Paris, France conjures up images of fine restaurants and romance. I say Phoenix and you feel hot and dry weather and envision a particular species of cactus. And on we could go, Chicago, San Francisco, Detroit. Certain cities call to mind specific ideals and images.

In the ancient world, Athens meant culture, architecture, education, philosophy. Athens, in Paul's day, however, had lost some of its sparkle. But it still had a reputation from the past when the lights of Aristotle, Plato, and Socrates had shined. A lot of history and a lot of art. Two thousand years later the Parthenon is still "visually satisfying." Athens, in Paul's day, as in ours, was a museum for the grandeur of Greek culture.

All of this is background, and Luke paints quite a picture in the six short verses of Acts 17:16-21. Luke mentions the Areopagus, that low hill in Athens with stone seats for the political council that met there. But, the philosophers upon whom he trains our eyes are the Epicureans and Stoics. The Epicureans had been around since 300 BC, and for them sense perception was the only basis for knowledge. The Epicureans were often attacked as atheists because they were opposed to the fear of death and to the fear of gods. They said, when we die we become like atoms, dissolved into the air like Alkaseltzer in water. Plop, plop, fizz, fizz, and we're gone! Epicureans had no hope for the afterlife.

The Stoics were best known for their emphasis on moral conduct. The only way to control life was to control passion. They thought that self control was the path to freedom. Like the Epicureans, the Stoics had no hope for life after death. Luke's picture is completed with the generalization that the Athenians were entertained by listening to "new ideas" (vss. 19, 21). This is the cultural milieu Luke imagines for us.

If you had six verses, which is all that Luke takes, how would you describe our society? how would you describe the culture in which we live? I asked that very question to an adult

Sunday School class. Their descriptions were images of agitation. One said, "We are pleasure seekers." Another said, "We're self absorbed." Yet another student cited one of the best selling books he'd seen on Oprah: *Be As Rich as You Want to Be.* Another painted this image of today's American: A single mother standing in line at 7 Eleven to buy a lottery ticket. These are negative images formed from agitated spirits. Finally, an older student summed up his picture of our culture with this statement, 'Detroit still hasn't recovered from the '67 riots and now we're erecting casinos to stimulate growth!" He was really provoked!

Paul's situation in Athens was pretty negative, too. The city was full of idols and Paul's spirit was provoked (v.16). He was agitated. And yet, notice how positive Paul sounds when he takes the opportunity to talk. He commends the Athenians as "very religious" (v. 22). Paul compliments their literature with this citation, "As some of your own poets have said…" (v. 28). Paul almost compliments one altar, "To an unknown god…" (v. 23). For an agitated spirit this is positive conversation.

Paul is most optimistic when he moves through the content of his sermon: God is the creator (v. 24), God is independent (v. 24-25), God is the source of all (v. 25), God is close yet far off (v. 26-27), God is our father (v.28). The philosophers in Paul's audience must have loved Paul's comments. Imagine the philosophers verbally responding, "uh-huh…yes…well…" They nod their approval because Paul affirms their reality. Positive responses until Paul comes to a point where he moves away from common beliefs. The rub comes with Paul's comment on the resurrection of Jesus (v. 31). Some believed. Others sneered. The Epicureans didn't believe in the resurrection of the dead. The Stoics didn't believe in the resurrection.

We are so much like Paul in non-Christian Athens. We live in a non-Christian land. Paul lived in a pre-Christian city. We live in a post- Christian country. We've shared Paul's agitated spirit when we consider the impassive witness of AIDS and Oklahoma City, the gambling and poverty in our city, and everywhere children starved for food and starved for love. Yes, we feel Paul's agitation over the pathetic condition of our society.

But, in our response to this culture of ours, it's not so easy to imitate the response of Paul. We've tended to react in one of two extremes. On the one hand, we've made a fuss, an entirely negative response, about matters that have no ultimate meaning. When I was young some folk concerned themselves with the length of men's hair, the length of women's skirts, and rock music. Twenty-five years later we've come to understand the folly of focusing on these trivial pursuits. But, nothing has changed. Only the topics have evolved. Prayer postures, song books, and clapping hands have now captured congregations' attentions. Could Satan have invented more effective distractions from the important issues of the day? We're examining the paint of the wall on the ship's cabin while the Titanic sinks!

On the other extreme, we've tried to blend in–altogether. To live a life so that no one knows we follow Jesus Christ. We live incognito, like green bugs on a green tree. So, nobody sees us. There is nothing in our language, nothing in our world view, nothing in our hopes, nothing in our dreams, nothing in how we spend our money, nothing in how we treat other people that sets us apart as a people who live with God.

How does Paul respond? Paul recognizes Athenian culture and Athenian beliefs as a legitimate conversation partner in talking about God. Paul doesn't condemn "the poets among you." Paul says the Greeks "groped after God" through their statues, and poetry and philosophy. For Paul, the Athenian religions laid a foundation for hearing about "the Lord of Heaven and earth." Paul is not silent and Paul does not focus on petty disputes. He picks up the beat in an intelligent conversation. Paul recognizes the rhythm and enters in at precisely the right moment. Oh, that we had such timing. Oh, that we had the skill to recognize the beat!

I received an e-mail last month from an old church friend. I hadn't heard from him in almost seven years but I knew he had been struggling with his faith. He had had no conversation partners. His church was too busy debating whether to have baby showers for the unwed. His church spent their time arguing the wisdom of restoring an old church bus. There was no time or place to talk about cultural issues that affected my friend. The church watched the paint dry on the cabin walls as my friend sank.

In his e-mail he wrote, "Somewhere along the way I lost my faith in Christianity. Emily [Dickinson] puts it bleakly

'To lose one's faith surpasses
The loss of an estate
Because estates can be
Replenished–faith cannot.
Inherited with life,
Belief but once can be;
Annihilate a single clause,
And Being's beggary.'"

Part of my friend's "case" was the narrow and misplaced focus of the Church of Christ and Evangelical Christianity. He had no dialogue partners for his concerns over peace and justice, the environment or feeding the hungry.

We are beginning to realize that we live in a post-Christian society. Recently a woman wrote of her post Christian experience. She had been raised in church but now, as a young adult, she finds her spirituality communing amongst nature. When given the opportunity to choose, she chose not to spend her Sunday morning at a cold stone church with its granite altar, blue carpet and irrelevant message. Now she exercises her spirit on long runs amidst tall trees that form a natural arch over the carpet of red and gold leaves. She runs through the forest to a bench that marks the summit of her run. From this vista she witnesses, in Easter-like fashion, a glorious sunrise. She testifies, "Standing there on the wooden bench, I am filled with a deep and quiet joy. I feel a reverence for life, a faith in mankind, a charity toward others. Standing there, witnessing the miraculous birth of a new day, I feel a connection to my creator–a connection that perhaps others feel in the old stone church."[4] We live in a post-Christian society. For many, church is a memory, a literary and spiritual springboard to reality. But, above the observations from mountain vistas and forest floors, is there not a reality of broader significance?

What do we say to this? What would Paul say? Paul would not hide nor would he focus on small minded matters. Paul engaged his culture on the macro level. Paul picked up the longings of Athenian religions and directed them to Jesus. Paul did not quote scripture to the Athenians who had no interaction

---

[4] Jessa Vartanian, "Running Religiously," *Runner's World*, (September, 1996) : 104.

with Judaism. Instead he appealed to their knowledge of creation and to our common humanity. Paul's God "made the world and all that is in it" (v. 24). Paul's God could "not be captured by buildings" (v. 24). Our true purpose, Paul said, is in God's service (v. 28-29).

What do we say? Where do we start? Who is this society of ours? Detroit sits now in the shadows of the million-dollar-a-day casinos. Motor City Casino shades the sun in this city. But, in the inky shadows there are people groping for…something. What drives our selfishness? What drives our pleasure seeking? What pushes the poor into the lottery line? Beneath the image of selfishness and pleasure seeking and the woman spending grocery money on Powerball, are people looking for something. What? Don't they all deeply desire meaning in life? Don't we all deeply desire a reason for living? Don't we all long for purpose? Isn't that why women invest in their children, reading books to them at night? Isn't that why some volunteer at the public library or at Beaumont Hospital? Isn't a desire for purpose what motivates you to roll down your window and stuff a dollar bill into the can of the Kiwanis collecting funds for the handicapped? Isn't a longing for meaning the reason we so approve of the local work training Leader Dogs for the blind? Isn't it a desire for purpose that causes you to volunteer in the Boy Scouts? We long for meaning in life!

Where do we start? What do we say? Paul begins with the natural world. Who can look into the stars and not see the designer? Who can survey the rugged Oregon coast, the brilliant turn of color in the Upper Peninsula, the first falling of fresh snow, and not know that there is a transcendent One who has sent these gifts? The Sunday runner feels a connection to her creator. She knows that God moves the galaxies and the tides. She looks for a conversation partner.

Not too long ago distinguished scholar Henry Louis Gates published his autobiography, *Colored People*.[5] Gates is the current chair of Afro-American studies at Harvard. He is an American intellectual. His book is a reflective journey of faith with a deep respect for church. During Gates' adolescence a visiting minister responded to Gates' burgeoning mind and

[5] Henry Louis Gates, Jr. Colored People: A Memoir (NY: Alfred A. Knopf, 1994).

challenging questions. The minister created a home in his denomination for young Henry Gates. Gates ultimately engaged a religious institution that reflected his whole person, his intelligence and race. He found a conversation partner.

Where do we start? What do we say? In our Western Society there exists a growing interest in the spiritual. Angels, new age spirituality, interest in beads and crystals, and the third wave of the charismatic movement. People are searching. People know that to make sense out of life, to give coherence to the world, they need something more. Paul does not roll his eyes in righteous indignation. He knows that they know, to paraphrase Augustine, that each person has a God shaped void within. Within each human being there is an emptiness that only God can fill. Paul knows that his audience knows, to paraphrase the Apostle John, that all persons are thirsty with a thirst that can only be quenched by Jesus.

There exists a God who loves us, who came to this earth in Jesus Christ. That is the central teaching of Christianity. When Paul left Athens and went off to Corinth, he later wrote back and said, "I knew nothing but Jesus Christ and him crucified." (1 Corinthians 2:2). That's what he knew in Athens. But, that's not all he knew. He knew his culture. He knew, for the woman running through the woods, for the man in the lottery line, for the woman rolling down her window to give a dollar for the blind, that ultimate fulfillment is in Jesus Christ.